DELIVERANCE FROM EVIL SPIRITS

Deliverance From Evil Spirits

A Weapon for Spiritual Warfare

Michael Scanlan, T.O.R.
Randall J. Cirner

Servant Books
Ann Arbor, Michigan

Copyright © 1980 by Michael Scanlan and Randall J. Cirner
Published by Servant Books, Box 8617, Ann Arbor, Michigan
48107
Cover and Book design by John B. Leidy

Nothing Contrary to Faith: Rev. Christian Oravec, T.O.R., S.T.D.
           Rev. Daniel Sinisi, T.O.R., M.A.,
           S.T.D.

Approved: Very Rev. Edmund Carroll, T.O.R.
      Minister Provincial

Printed in the United States of America

ISBN 0-89283-091-3

Contents

PREFACE

The last ten years have seen a barrage of books which can be classified under the general category of deliverance. The term "deliverance" is used here in a generic sense to refer to any confrontation with an evil spirit aimed at overcoming his influence. Deliverance, then, can encompass the whole range of encounters with evil spirits, from repulsing satanic temptation to exorcising a possessed person. Most of these books have been popular ones written mainly by Protestant neo-pentecostals and aimed at acquainting people with deliverance. Other authors have taken a more scholarly approach, and have investigated the biblical, theological, and patristic materials regarding the existence and role of Satan and evil spirits.

This book is based on the more than ten years experience that we have both had in pastoral care and in praying with people for deliverance. During these ten years, we have read the scholarly and popular works and, in addition, have done much research on our own. While the literature is diverse and at times extreme, our conclusion is that there is a sound basis in scripture, theology, and Christian tradition for the exercise of what is called deliverance. In this book, we try to give the reader a sufficient foundation in scripture and tradition for understanding deliverance in the context of spiritual warfare, but our main purpose is to set the exercise of this ministry in its proper context—that of pastoral care.

While we hope that anyone who reads this book will find it interesting and useful, it is intended mainly for those who are engaged in the pastoral care of committed groups of Christians. We believe that deliverance has its role primarily within the context of overall pastoral care. We also believe that deliverance is most effective within this context. We maintain that the preparation, ministry, and follow-up necessary for deliverance can take place only where there is sufficient commitment, responsibility, authority, and accountability among Christians. Such elements guard against many of the abuses so often associated with deliverance, and they clearly situate the responsibility for the exercise of the ministry within a given pastoral structure.

The pastoral model we present in Chapter Seven does not presuppose a certain pastoral structure. This model can be employed in a variety of pastoral structures: parishes, congregations, covenant communities. What is important is that there be sufficient commitment, responsibility, authority, and accountability to insure that the important elements of the pastoral model are effectively established.

We also discuss self-deliverance and other situations in which it is necessary to deal with evil spirits, but where the pastoral model itself does not immediately apply. However, we still maintain that deliverance should operate within a pastoral structure even in these situations.

In this book, we make a strong statement about the nature and purpose of satanic activity. Our intention is to show the range of such activity. To do so, we will examine the scriptures, patristic sources, contemporary writings, and our own extensive experience in praying with people for deliverance. Our purpose is to help those with pastoral responsibility realize that many of the problems and difficulties in people's lives can be the work of evil spirits.

In order to emphasize this point, we decided not to follow each assertion that a particular problem can be the work of evil spirits with a qualifying statement that the particular problem might also have other sources. We make this qualification periodically, but we do not say it all the time. This does not mean that we are the victims of a "devil mania" which sees evil spirits as the cause of everything that goes wrong in life. To the contrary, we want to state firmly and clearly that evil spirits are not always, nor even primarily, the source of people's difficulties.

Man's fallen nature (the flesh), and that system of things in the material order opposed to God (the world), are ready sources of sin and disorder for the Christian. Temptation, mental disorders, physical illness, emotional problems, in short, all of the afflictions we mention in this book, can and are caused by our human condition and our environment as well as by evil spirits. In this regard, we acknowledge the important role the social sciences play in helping us understand human behavior. In fact, Chapter Nine includes a short essay by a clinical psychologist who has reviewed this manuscript from his professional perspective.

Deliverance will not solve problems which are caused by something other than evil spirits. Therefore, it is crucial to determine the correct origin of the problem in each case and deal with it accordingly. In the examples we present in this book, the conclusion that an evil spirit was the cause was usually arrived at through discussion, experience, and discernment. In a few examples, we show how revelation by the Holy Spirit unmasked an evil spirit. But in each instance, we judged each case on its own merits and found the problem to be the result of demonic activity. We did not simply assume this because of a preexisting mind set on our part.

It is also important to note the emphasis we place on a positive approach to the Christian life. No amount of deliverance can replace the central need in a person's life to accept the lordship of Jesus and to live out the reality of that commitment in concrete terms. Deliverance is a gift which helps men and women to live an aggressive and effective Christian life. Getting freed from evil spirits is not an end in itself, but is a means to the end. The end is union with God, life with brothers and sisters, and preaching the gospel.

ONE

The Kingdom of God

In order to understand the concept of spiritual warfare, we must see it against the background of the biblical preaching of the kingdom of God. We will not be able to comprehend the reality of our situation until we see clearly the purpose of God as embodied in the context of the kingdom. The New Testament proclamation of the kingdom of God and the realities inherent in that proclamation utterly destroy the foundations for the bland Christianity so often preached today. The forcefulness and the violence with which Jesus confronted all that opposed the kingdom of God belies any notion that the Christian life is one of ease. In fact, Jesus tells his disciples that they can expect the same kind of life he himself had as they preach the kingdom (Mk 10:24,25).

The biblical proclamation of the kingdom of God can be distilled into four main ideas:

1. The reign of God has come into the world in the presence of Jesus.

2. All men can and must enter the kingdom of God in order to be saved.

3. The kingdom of God is destroying the kingdom of Satan.

4. The kingdom of God will be fully established and the kingdom of Satan eternally destroyed at the second coming of the Lord Jesus Christ.

Jesus and the Kingdom of God

By his very presence, and by what he said and did, Jesus inaugurated the kingdom of God on earth. His preaching and teaching attested to the fact that he was singularly and uniquely commissioned to speak words of God to men (Jn 7:46; Mt 7:29). His deeds of healing and miracles are a sure sign to John the Baptist that Jesus is indeed the Messiah, the Holy One of God who is to come (Lk 7:18-23). Jesus also claimed an authority which God alone possessed (Mk 2:5-7). Jesus identified God as his Father in a strong and unequivocal way which was bound to have its impact on the Jews (Jn 6). And if all else failed to convince those around him of his true nature and mission, there was one time when the veil was briefly thrown aside. It was no parable, no allusion which could be misunderstood, when Jesus boldly and plainly decreed to the Jews that "I am." (Jn 8:58).

The kingdom of God is not an earthly, territorially bounded kingdom (Jn 18:36). It is mainly a kingdom within a man which makes him a new creation (Jn 3:5). But the sons of the kingdom can be known quite easily because their actions (deeds) are different from those of the sons of the world (Mt 5:18). The kingdom of God is not just an internal reality, but an external one as well, attested to by the relationships seen among those who have entered the kingdom.

The kingdom is already present and men can experience the fruits of the kingdom in this life (Mt 10:7-13a). But it is not yet *fully* present. The kingdom of God awaits its full realization at the second coming of the Lord (Mt 13:36-43).

Jesus himself began his public ministry by proclaiming the arrival of the Kingdom of God and demonstrating its power through his healings and miracles (Mt 4:23). Jesus' teaching firmly established how one ought to live in the kingdom.

The Kingdom of Salvation

The proclamation of the arrival of the kingdom of God was a shattering event in human history. Jesus was not just another wise teacher who made his appearance and left his sayings as a source of inspiration for future disciples. The kingdom he proclaimed was not, and therefore is not, merely another alternative lifestyle which one can either accept or reject on the basis of personal preference, personality configuration, convenience, or cultural heritage. The central message of the kingdom cuts completely through such superficialities and speaks to man about his very life. The meaning of the kingdom, the message that it carries, is not determined by man but rather it determines man.

The message of the kingdom is one of salvation. It tells man that he has fallen from the relationship he once enjoyed with God and is incapable on his own of regaining it (Jn 8:24). Man has placed himself in bondage to sin; he is a slave to it (Jn 8:34). He is under the dominion of the "ruler of this world" (Jn 12:31). To sinful man, the kingdom proclaims an age of salvation through faith in Jesus Christ, the Son of God (Jn 3:16-17). It is a salvation that is available to all men everywhere (Lk 13:29). All men can enter the kingdom; in fact, all men *must* enter the kingdom in order to be saved. And the only means into the kingdom is acceptance of the Lord Jesus (Jn 14:6).

The kingdom of God is of the highest value; it is the most valuable thing a man can have (Mt 13:45-46). It is worth risking everything to possess the kingdom, even one's very life, because only in the kingdom of God can a man truly find his life (Lk 10:34-39). Therefore, the kingdom of God is made up of those who have come to the Lord and have been brought out of bondage to the elements of the kingdom of darkness and freed from enslavement to the ruler of that kingdom, Satan.

The Two Kingdoms

In one sense it is inaccurate to speak of "two kingdoms"—the kingdom of God and the kingdom of Satan. Satan is assuredly not a god or spiritual force capable of independent activity. He is a creature of God and is subject to God's restraints in every way except that he possesses free will. Satan's hatred toward God and his enmity toward the children of God

were not created into him by God. Nor is Satan's malevolence
the result of some flaw in God's creation. It is, rather, the
result of Satan's pride and rebellion against God (2 Pt 2:4).

At the same time, however, the scriptures do clearly talk
about the kingdom of Satan which is antagonistic toward
God's kingdom (Mt 12:25-28). Satan's kingdom is the kingdom
of this world (Lk 4:5-6). In his enmity toward God, the ruler
of this kingdom wants to stifle the life of the kingdom of God
growing within men. Satan does so through his own personal
activity in the hearts of men (Mt 13:19), and also through the
people, ideas, and events which make up the kingdom of this
age (Mt 13:22).

The two kingdoms—God's and Satan's—exist side by side in
this world (Mt 13:38), and yet the two can be clearly distin-
guished because of their deeds (Jn 3:19-21).

It is this kingdom of Satan which the Son of God has come to
destroy (Jn 12:31). The Lord's very presence causes demons to
tremble and fear because they recognize in him the power and
authority of God, and they know that God will not always
allow them the free hand they have enjoyed (Mk 1:23-24).

A major part of Jesus' public ministry was to cast out demons (Mk 1:34). In so doing, he announced the downfall of
Satan's kingdom. He is the stronger one who binds the strong
man and shows that power and authority belong to God alone.
The strong man has been bound and now his kingdom may be
plundered (Mt 12:29). Jesus clearly says that his power to exorcise evil spirits heralds the arrival of a greater and stronger
kingdom—the kingdom of God (Mt 12:28).

The Full Realization
of the Kingdom of God

The kingdom of God has indeed come into the world; it is a
source of daily strength for those who live in it, and it is the
source of salvation for those who respond to its call for conversion. By his death and resurrection, the Lord Jesus has decisively overthrown the kingdom of Satan. At the same time, we
are confronted with the fact that we do not yet enjoy the full-

ness of the kingdom of God. There is still a pain in our hearts because we do not yet see our Lord face to face. The small taste of the kingdom we have now makes us yearn for the day when the whole of creation will be fully restored, when all the sons and daughters of God will know the unending joy which has been prepared for them since the dawn of creation (Mt 25:34).

Furthermore, while we await the full realization of the kingdom of God, we are confronted by an even more stark reality—evil still abounds in the world. Its ultimate power and claim have been broken through Jesus Christ, but sin, sickness, and death still continue to affect the children of the kingdom (Jn 16:33).

The ruler of this world knows clearly his ultimate ruin is assured. Yet his struggle continues. He wants to sweep to destruction as much as he can before his power is forever taken from him (Rv 20:10). The devil continues to rule over the world of men opposed to God. He rules those who do not know the good news of the kingdom, and those who do know it but refuse to accept it (1 Jn 5:19).

Those who are not in the kingdom of God are surely the easier prey for Satan, but he directs his special wrath against children of the kingdom (Rv 12:17). The sons and daughters of the kingdom of God are living testimony to Satan's own ruin, and their power over him through the Holy Spirit can give freedom to all men and women (Lk 10:17,19). But because we live between the proclamation of the kingdom and its final completion, we must be careful how we live (Jn 17:15). For the Lord will return quickly at an unexpected time and bring to completion what he began on earth (Mt 24:44).

This fact—that we live between the initial coming of the kingdom of God and its full and final establishment—brings us to the heart of spiritual warfare.

When Jesus left the earth, he gave a monumental task to those already in his kingdom—to "make disciples of all nations" (Mt 28:19,20). The kingdom of God is to be an inclusive one. All men need to know about it and receive it. The followers of the Lord Jesus are to extend his kingdom to "the ends of the earth." In other words, Jesus' followers are not to spend the period of time until the Lord returns in idle waiting. Those who have been brought to new life in Jesus must carry on his mission. Jesus himself was sent by the Father and he in turn sends his disciples (Jn 20:21).

The task Jesus gave his disciples of spreading the kingdom can be best expressed under two main categories: preaching (or proclaiming the gospel to others) and loving one another.

The gospel needs to be proclaimed. People must hear about the need for repentance from sin, and the need to accept Jesus Christ as Lord. They must hear that God's love and call extend to them, and that the emptiness of their lives can only be filled by God himself. Jesus' disciples cannot afford to wait for the world to come to them. Most people in the world do not even know what they need. It is up to God's people to tell the world what it needs and how to get it.

The proclamation of the kingdom must be accompanied by a clear demonstration of the kingdom. It is notable that during his last few hours with his disciples Jesus was most concerned about the way they love one another. Chapters 12-17 of John's Gospel are filled with his teaching about this. Jesus commands his disciples to love one another (Jn 13:34), and he prays to the Father for the love and unity of his disciples (Jn 17:23). The life of the kingdom consists of loving one another, and that love is a sure sign to others that what has been preached to them is true (Jn 13:35).

This twofold commission—to proclaim the gospel and to love one another—provides the framework to understand Satan's twofold strategy: to keep man in bondage to sin and to the world, thus keeping them from the kingdom of God entirely; and to render ineffective, in any way possible, those who are already in God's kingdom. The first activity is directed at those who are not Christians. The second is directed at those who are.

St. Justin Martyr, one of the early Christian apologists, put it this way:

These spirits whom we call demons strive for nothing else than to alienate men from God their Creator, and from Christ, His first-begotten. Indeed, they have clamped down those who are powerless to lift themselves above earthly conditions, and they still clamp them down to earthly things, and to manufactured idols. Besides, they even try to trip those who rise to the contemplation of divine things, and, unless such persons are wise in their judgments and pure and passionless in their life, the demons will force them into ungodliness.[1]

God desires that men and women come to him; receive his love, forgiveness, and abundant life; and share in the very life of God by becoming a member of his family. Satan desires that men and women be in complete bondage to Satan himself through bondage to the world and sin. Ultimately, this bondage leads to eternal death in hell.

These two purposes are completely inimical to one another. There is no room for compromise, no basis for peaceful coexistence. There can be only struggle and opposition. For the light and truth and righteousness of the kingdom of God can have nothing to do with the lies and darkness and sin of the kingdom of Satan. We live in an interim period between the mortal blow dealt to Satan by the cross and the final destruction of his kingdom when the Lord comes again. During this interim period, God calls his people to attack the kingdom of darkness and to further the kingdom of light. Man is born into the midst of this struggle; by its very nature he *must* fight in it. No one can escape from it. Every man and woman must choose whom they will serve.

TWO

Spiritual Warfare

In the late 1960s, when Christians in the main-line denominations were first baptized in the Holy Spirit on a large scale, one of the most frequent comments about this experience was, "I now know God personally in a way I never did before." The knowledge and experience of the close, personal love of God is one of the chief effects of being baptized in the Holy Spirit. This renewed contact with God brought with it a deeper and richer prayer life, the exercise of the spiritual gifts, a new understanding of and love for the scriptures, and for those with sacramental traditions, a realization of the meaning and importance of the sacraments. For those of us involved in the charismatic renewal, it seemed that we were suddenly immersed in the things of the Spirit in a way we thought was reserved only for a few privileged people.

We also realized that the spiritual realm included spiritual forces hostile to God and hostile to us, his people. Early prophecies in the charismatic renewal spoke mainly of God's love for us and his desire to draw us ever closer to himself. But prophecies also warned us to beware of the devil and to guard ourselves against his work. In fact, those very things which had come alive for us and enriched our relationship with God— prayer, scripture, the sacraments, the historic truths of the Church—all served to remind us of the fact that Satan was alive. We had to face a malevolent personal being, unalterably and completely opposed to God, to God's people, and to God's

plan for the world. In short, at the same time that we redis-
covered and renewed our relationship with God, we also redis-
covered our relationship with Satan.

Those who want to live a fruitful and effective Christian life
must recognize the satanic reality where it exists and defeat it
in the power and authority of the Lord. One of the great difficulties the Christian Church faces today is that many Christians simply do not acknowledge that Satan and evil spirits
exist. Some dismiss the devil as a rather gruesome medieval
myth, the whipping boy of a superstitious and entrenched hier-
archy trying to control the equally superstitious mass of ordinary Christians. Others regard the devil as an archetypical
"symbol" of the evil that human beings are capable of, a symbol that allows man to avoid personal responsibility for what
he does. Hence, "the devil made me do it." For a dwindling
number, the devil does exist but as a distant force, someone
whom only God and the saints need to be concerned about.

These views are false. They are also highly convenient for
Satan's activity. Behind the twin smokescreens of unbelief and
ignorance, Satan is able to entangle the affairs of men and the
Church in cleverly devised snares, bringing many men and
women to ruin and rendering whole segments of the Christian
Church ineffective.

The fact is that many Christians do not live in the full freedom of the sons and daughters of God because many areas of
their lives are in bondage to Satan. Sins, unwanted habits,
physical illness, emotional wounds, psychological problems,
"bad luck," disunity in relationships, problems in relating to
God, fears, and compulsions are just some of the ways Satan
wages war against the children of God.

Nothing is too small or too large, too human or too spiritual
to escape Satan's attention. From the daily events of our personal lives to the complex workings of huge governments and
organizations, Satan and his evil spirits find ways to infect the
world and the Church.

The key question for many people about spiritual warfare is:
Does the devil actually exist? Can we know for certain that
there are such entities as evil spirits? Ultimately, these questions find their answer in one way—through revelation.

Revelation

Man's own observations and ideas will carry him only part of the way into the question of the existence of Satan and evil spirits. His own observations of the world might lead him to conclude that man has a native desire to do wrong, or that man is basically good, but his wrongdoing is the result of social factors which need to be brought under more control. Perhaps he may even conclude that there are "spiritual forces" at work which can determine the course of the affairs of men.

On the one hand, all of these conclusions could have some validity, and an individual could try to live his life according to one of these conclusions. But the conclusion is still a conjecture. The only way man can actually know his true condition and the ultimate spiritual realities of the world around him is if God reveals these things to him. Christians accept the fact that God is the one who can show them such ultimate truth and reality about their lives.

Thus the way Christians can be sure of the existence and activity of Satan and evil spirits is through revelation. God has to say that such beings do exist.

But how do we know what God has said about evil spirits? For the answer we must turn to God's word to us through scripture. For those who are Catholics, there is the additional help that the official teaching office of the Catholic Church can, and does, authoritatively interpret what the scriptures say.

While there is clear teaching in scripture that Satan and evil spirits do exist, scripture does not state precisely where they came from or how they came to oppose God. However, the broad facts are clear enough. Three passages in the New Testament say that evil spirits are angels who sinned and were cast into hell:

For if God did not spare the angels when they sinned, but cast them into hell and committed them to pits of nether gloom to be kept until the judgment... (2 Pt 2:4)

The letter of Jude makes essentially the same point in verse 6:

And the angels that did not keep their own position but left their proper dwelling have been kept by him in eternal chains in the nether gloom until the judgment of the great day.

And in Revelation:

Now war arose in heaven, Michael and his angels fighting against the dragon; and the dragon and his angels fought, but they were defeated and there was no longer any place for them in heaven. And the great dragon was thrown down, that ancient serpent, who is called the Devil and Satan, the deceiver of the whole world—he was thrown down to the earth, and his angels were thrown down with him. And I heard a loud voice in heaven, saying,

"Now the salvation and the power and the kingdom of our God and the authority of his Christ have come, for the accuser of our brethren has been thrown down, who accuses them day and night before our God. And they have conquered him by the blood of the Lamb and by the word of their testimony, for they loved not their lives even unto death. Rejoice then, O heaven and you that dwell therein! But woe to you, O earth and sea, for the devil has come down to you in great wrath, because he knows that his time is short!" (Rv 12:7-12)

These three passages from the New Testament, coupled with a passage about the fall of the king of Babylon in Isaiah (14:12-15), have formed the basis for the Church Fathers' statement that Satan and his evil spirits were angels who lost their place in heaven through sin. The sin is usually described as pride.

Origen puts it this way:

In regard to the devil and his angels and opposing powers, the ecclesiastical teaching maintains that these beings do indeed exist; but what they are or how they exist is not explained with sufficient clarity. This opinion, however, is held by most: that the devil was an angel; and having apostasized, he persuaded as many angels as possible to fall away with himself; and these, even to the present time, are called his angels.[2]

What is interesting to note is that Origen states that the nature and beginning of Satan and evil spirits is unclear. However, he says that the constant teaching of the early Church, based on the scriptures, is that Satan and evil spirits do exist.

The New Testament contains God's clear and unequivocal revelation about the existence of evil spirits and their evil intentions. Peter says that our "adversary the devil prowls around like a roaring lion seeking someone to devour" (1 Pt 5:8). Paul says in Ephesians that we are at war "against the principalities, against the powers, against the world rulers of this present darkness, against the spiritual hosts of wickedness in the heavenly places" (Eph 6:12). John says, "The reason the Son of God appeared was to destroy the works of the devil" (1 Jn 3:8).

As mentioned earlier, overcoming the work of Satan and his evil spirits is a central theme in the ministry of Jesus. The Lord began his public ministry after having first had a dramatic encounter with Satan in the desert. His decisive victory over every personal temptation of the devil in the desert set the stage for the final victory Jesus won for all on the cross. In the desert, Jesus defeated Satan personally. During his public ministry he defeated Satan's hold on individuals. On the cross he won victory for all who want it.

The list of New Testament passages which speak of the existence and activity of Satan and evil spirits is impressive. The very number of such passages makes the message of scripture clear and consistent. A list of these passages is included in the appendix to this book.

Tradition

We find the teaching of the Church Fathers to be in harmony with the scriptures. The following quotes are from the writings of Cyprian, Irenaeus, and Tertullian:

For the rest, what else is waged daily in the world but a battle against the devil, but a struggle with continual onsets against his darts and weapons.[3]

As to the Devil, he as being an Apostate Angel, hath that power only, which he discloses in the beginning—to seduce and withdraw man's mind unto transgression of God's commandments, and gradually to blind the hearts of such as make it their business to serve him, to the forgetting of the true God, and the worshipping of Satan himself as God.[4]

Their business is to corrupt mankind; thus, the spirit of evil was from the very beginning bent upon man's destruction. The demons, therefore, inflict upon men's bodies diseases and other bitter misfortunes, and upon the soul sudden and extraordinary outbursts of violence.[5]

The writings of the Protestant reformers maintain the scriptural and patristic teaching about evil spirits. John Calvin, for instance, teaches that Christians wage an irreconcilable struggle against satanic forces:

The fact that the devil is everywhere called God's adversary and ours also ought to fire us to an unceasing struggle against him. For if we have God's glory at heart, as we should have, we ought with all our strength to contend against him who is trying to extinguish it. If we are minded to affirm Christ's Kingdom as we ought, we must wage irreconcilable war with him who is plotting its ruin. Again, if we care about our salvation at all, we ought to have neither peace nor truce with him who continually lays traps to destroy it. So, indeed, is he described in Genesis 3, where he seduces man from the obedience owed to God, that he may simultaneously deprive God of his due honor and hurl man himself into ruin (vs. 1-5). So, also, in the Evangelists, where he is called "an enemy" (Mt 13:28,39), and is said to sow weeds in order to corrupt the seed of eternal life (Mt 13:25). In sum, we experience in all of Satan's deeds what Christ testifies concerning him, that "from the beginning he was a murderer...and a liar" (Jn 8:44). For he opposes the truth of God with falsehoods, he obscures the light with darkness, he entangles men's minds in errors, he stirs up hatred, he kindles contentions and combats, everything to the end that he may overturn God's Kingdom and plunge men with himself into eternal death. From this it appears that he is in nature depraved, evil, and malicious. For there must be consummate depravity in that disposition which devotes itself to assailing God's glory and man's salvation. This, also, is what John means in his letter, when he writes that "the devil has sinned from the beginning" (1 Jn 3:8). Indeed, he considers him as the author, leader, and architect of all malice and iniquity.[6]

Contemporary Sources

Also, in the last decade of our own century, the Catholic Church has upheld that denomination's belief in the existence and influence of Satan and demons.

Pope Paul VI, in a General Audience in November, 1973, spoke strongly of the evil inflicted upon the Church and the world by the devil:

What are the greatest needs of the Church today?

Do not let our answer surprise you as being oversimple or even superstitious and unreal: one of the greatest needs is defense from that evil which is called the Devil.

Pope Paul continued:

So we know that this dark and disturbing spirit really exists, and that he still acts with treacherous cunning; he is the secret enemy that sows errors and misfortunes in human history. We should recall the revealing evangelical parable of the wheat and the weeds, the synthesis and explanation of the illogicality that seems to preside over our conflicting vicissitudes: "inimicus homo hoc fecit" (Mt 13:28). He was "a murderer from the beginning...and the father of lies," as

Christ defines him (Jn 8:44-45); he launches sophistic attacks on the moral equilibrium of man. He is the treacherous and cunning enchanter who finds his way into us by way of the senses, the imagination, the lust, utopian logic, or disorderly social contacts in the give-and-take of life, to introduce deviations, as harmful as they are apparently in conformity with our physical of psychical structures, or our deep, instinctive aspirations.

This question of the Devil and the influence he can exert on individual persons as well as on communities, whole societies, or events, is a very important chapter of Catholic doctrine which is given little attention today, though it should be studied again.[7]

In the Anglican Church, we have the conclusions of a commission established by the Anglican bishop of Exeter, England, to study the question of exorcism in the New Testament.

It is clear that the primitive preaching (e.g. of Peter, in Acts 10:38) gave as one of the chief characteristics of the mission of Christ the fact that he freed men from the power of the devil. Paul, when exorcizing Elymas the sorcerer, called him a son of the devil (Acts 13:10). The primitive catechesis, which can be seen in 1 Pt 5:8, Jas 4:7, and Eph 4:27 and 6:11, called upon new Christians to resist the devil whom they renounced at baptism. "Before we believed in God," says the Epistle of Barnabas (16:7), "our house was a house of devils . . . but when we received remission of our sins and hoped in the Name, we became new." A later document (1 Jn 3:8-10) reaffirms the early view: "He that doth sin is of the devil, because the devil sinneth from the beginning. To this end was the Son of God made manifest, that he might undo the works of the devil."

It might be thought that all this was so much metaphorical language used to describe the passions of men and their effect in the world, but the direct claim made in 1 John 5:19 and John 17:15 rejects this. The world is indeed a wicked place but that is because it lies in the power of the devil.

One cannot get away from the fact that the New Testament is teaching a personal origin for evil; it simply will not do to dismiss this language as metaphor. It was against such a background that the gospel narratives of particular exorcisms by Christ were composed. Now it is sometimes the fashion to treat these narratives as if they were accommodations to the popular belief of the age, that things did not happen in the way they are narrated, but that the language of Christ, e.g. when he healed the woman bent double (Luke 13:16), attributed her curvature to Satan simply because that was what people expected of him to say and he did not want to undeceive them. Yet this principle of accommodation, recognized by patristic Scripture scholars such as St. John Chrysostom, while it justifies one in supposing that God did not trouble to enlighten the prophets about matters of physical science but let them go bumbling on in their ignorance, cannot on any reasonable view of God's action in revelation be extended to matters which are of import to salvation. If one were to hold that misleading language on the part of Luke, or of Christ himself, about what Satan had done to the bent woman did not matter, and if one were to conclude that the existence or nonexistence of the devil did not matter to the salvation of mankind, then it would be pertinent to ask what really does matter to that end. One might suggest that in so important an affair the motive of insuring oneself against the possibility that Satan does exist ought to be an important consideration. This particular incident can hardly be made to fit the theories of those who claim that gospel language about the devil is metaphorical. Their favorite gambit is to say that it is the wrath of God towards sinful man that is being covered by the metaphor of the devil, but in that case why was an innocent woman its victim?[8]

The Exeter Commission squarely faces one of the most important questions in determining the evidence for Satan, evil spirits, and possession in the scriptures. That is, can the New Testament stories of Jesus' exorcisms be taken literally, or are they metaphors? Some hold that Jesus was simply going along with the popular thinking of the time which held that demons were behind such things as epilepsy, insanity, and other forms of abnormal behavior as well as certain illnesses. Jesus, not wishing to upset such a view, "exorcised" people, but the demons he drove out were for him not discrete entities but metaphors for the social, psychological, or physical evil that was present.

The German Jesuit, Adolf Rodewyk, replies to such a theory in much the same way as the Exeter Commission.

> References to possessed persons in the Gospels are numerous—all told, about fifty cases—in referring to Christ's powers of exorcism. Recent interpreters have suggested that Jesus did not actually drive out devils, but only pretended to do so, in order to go along with prevailing folk beliefs; this would be in line with his failure to correct other erroneous views, such as that the sun circles the earth.
>
> We should, however, be aware of the basic difference between Christ's tolerance of erroneous views in the natural sciences and those in the field of religion. He did not regard it as one of his tasks to enlighten mankind on purely natural, physical conditions of their environment; this was outside the task he had been given by his Father. He had joined mankind in order to instruct it in the field of religion. He had come to establish the Kingdom of God and to eliminate the rule of Satan. John says this quite clearly: "It was to undo all that the devil has done that the son of God appeared" (Jn 3:8). Satan had been able to achieve a great deal just because he had managed to hide and disguise himself. This was made easier because he was a spirit, invisible to physical view. He was behind many events in which men did not suspect him, and even when they did recognize or suspect him, they were helpless and did not know how to deal with him. It was on this aspect of existence that Christ did not leave man in doubt or without help. Here he spoke and acted clearly.
>
> It is hardly necessary to note that with Christ there could

be no error. As the Son of God, he commanded infallible insight. Thus, when he insisted that someone had an evil spirit—meaning that he was possessed—we are dealing with an unfailingly correct diagnosis that cannot be touched by any objections whatever. When we are dealing with the Gospel accounts, therefore, detailing Christ's exorcisms, it basically does not matter whether the devil pulled the possessed victim hither and yon or did whatever else with him; the main thing is that Christ, in such a case, recognized the Devil and dealt with him accordingly.

Jesus clearly differentiated between possession and disease. He told his disciples, when he first sent them into the world, "Cure the sick...cast out devils" (Mt 10:8). Later, when he passed on to them his power to drive out devils, he says, "In my name they will cast out devils . . . they will lay their hands on the sick" (Mk 16:17-18). The Gospels put it in similar terms. Matthew introduces the report on the choice of the Apostles with these words: "He summoned his twelve disciples, and gave them the authority over unclean spirits with power to cast them out and to cure all kinds of diseases and sickness" (Mt 10:1). From the start, Mark summarized Christ's miracles as follows: "He cured many who were suffering from diseases of one kind or another; he also cast out many devils" (Mk 1:34).

In his activities, Jesus differentiated clearly between abnormal disturbances caused by illness and those caused by possession. This becomes obvious from the different ways in which he dealt with two who were deaf and dumb. One he "took aside in private, away from the crowd, put his fingers into the man's ears and touched his tongue with spittle . . . and he said to him, 'Ephphatha,' that is, 'Be opened.' And his ears were opened, and the ligament of his tongue was loosened and he spoke clearly" (Mk 7:33-35).

But in the second case, that of the deaf and dumb boy, Jesus said: "Deaf and dumb spirit . . . I command you: come out of him and never enter him again" (Mk 9:25-26). The Gospel might well have related this incident with words identical to those used by Matthew for a third case: "They had only just left when a man was brought to him, a dumb demoniac. And when the devil was cast out, the dumb man spoke, and the people were amazed" (Mt 9:32-34).

If these three cases had been taken to a modern physician, such as a nose, ear, and throat specialist, he might well have shrugged his shoulders in both cases, saying simply, "He is deaf and dumb, and he can't be helped." He would hardly have assumed that two entirely different causes were at the bottom of these clinical symptoms, and that two entirely different methods of cure had to be considered. Christ acted differently![9]

Once the existence of evil spirits has been established, it's important to understand the relevance of the fact. It is possible to acknowledge that such entities do exist, but at the same time to deny that evil spirits have any real effect on one's life. Indeed, for most people, the fact of the existence of evil spirits has about as much personal meaning as do the black holes in space. But as the above citations indicate, it is crucial to confront the significance that evil spirits have for Christians' lives.

The teaching of scripture on the matter is very clear. In fact, it paints a rather awesome picture:

> Be sober, be watchful. Your adversary the devil prowls around like a roaring lion, seeking someone to devour. Resist him, firm in your faith, knowing that the same experience of suffering is required of your brotherhood throughout the world. (1 Pt 5:8-9)

> Finally, be strong in the Lord and in the strength of his might. Put on the whole armor of God, that you may be able to stand against the wiles of the devil.
>
> For we are not contending against flesh and blood, but against the principalities, against the powers, against the world rulers of this present darkness, against the spiritual hosts of wickedness in the heavenly places. Therefore take the whole armor of God, that you may be able to withstand in the evil day, and having done all, to stand. Stand there-

fore, having girded your loins with truth, and having put on the breastplate of righteousness, and having shod your feet with the equipment of the gospel of peace; above all taking the shield of faith, with which you can quench all the flaming darts of the evil one. And take the helmet of salvation, and the sword of the Spirit, which is the word of God. Pray at all times in the Spirit, with all prayer and supplication. To that end keep alert with all perseverance, making supplication for all the saints, and also for me, that utterance may be given me in opening my mouth boldly to proclaim the mystery of the gospel . . . (Eph 6:10-19)

This is no soft Christianity in which one basks in the comfortable sunshine of a trouble-free life. Quite the opposite is the case. The Christian life is one of struggle and conflict. Satan is totally and irreconcilably opposed to the children of God. As surely as a lion goes about the forests and fields in search of food, so Christians can expect that the devil is stalking them.

One reason why many Christians cannot conceptualize the hostility which Satan has toward them is that modern Western culture puts a very high premium on such things as mutual understanding, dialogue, compromise, and individual expression. These are based on a concept of pluralism which insures that everyone can do what they want and think as they please. What is important is not that there be agreement about things but that we understand where each is "coming from." Through understanding, people become tolerant of the other's point of view and find that, in fact, they can live very happily side by side, while not agreeing about almost anything. These are the values Western man is taught; the people who embody such values become models for the rest of society.

Dialogue, compromise, and tolerance are important aspects of life. Without them man would find it very difficult to survive. The problem, as we see it, is that Western society has divinized them. The result is a myopic view of life which holds that everyone—indeed, reality itself—must be cooperative and tolerant. Thus the concept of an evil entity bent on one's total destruction doesn't find much room in Western thinking. The concept gets dismissed as lacking in logic, propriety, and the "modern way." Because Western man has decided that malevolent forces shouldn't exist he concludes that they actually do not exist. This way of thinking is dangerous.

This attitude is also apparent in many of those in Western culture who do allow for the existence of spiritual forces other than "God." These people tend to define these forces in terms readily acceptable to the modern way of thinking. Thus, many modern-day spiritists, spiritualists, witches, and warlocks claim that they are in touch with "good" spirits who only want to help mankind. These spiritual entities do not judge or coerce. To be sure, spiritists admit, a human being can misuse these spiritual powers for evil purposes. But, they say, this is a problem with man and not the spirits themselves. The spirits are basically good, or perhaps, neutral.

This claim is suspect. Many men and women who were converted to Christianity after being involved in the world of spiritism tell a different story. Their experiences in that world show that the so-called friendly spirits are in fact engaged in trapping people into their system, trying to make human beings dependent upon them for guidance, direction, favors, and good luck. Their real purpose is not to be of service to mankind but to trap men and women and enslave them to themselves. The claim that their activities are benevolent finds acceptance not because it is true, but because it fits the current value system so well.

The basic point here is a simple one. Western culture seems rather incapable of accepting the existence of a personal and incorrigible evil entity, but scripture says (as we have already seen), that evil entities do in fact exist. The Christian must look to the Lord for knowledge of the truth, and we must base our life on what the Lord says, not on what the latest cultural trend says.

THREE

How Evil Spirits Affect Mankind

Scripture doesn't give a complete list of the ways evil spirits affect man. The main intention of the writers of the gospels was not to catalogue all the activities of evil spirits, but rather to show that Jesus overcame the kingdom of Satan and exercised authority over evil spirits no matter where he found them. Nevertheless, the encounters between Jesus and Satan and evil spirits do give a picture of the ways the forces of evil operate in the world. Taking the scriptural accounts as a whole, satanic activity toward men can be categorized under three main headings: temptation, opposition, and bondage.

Temptation

Satan appears as the tempter at the very beginning of the human story. Through his seductions, Adam and Eve sinned and turned from God. This is Satan's basic purpose in temptation—to entice man to sin in order to hinder, block, and ultimately to sever his relationship with God. This was his object with Job. Satan wanted to put the kind of pressure on Job which would finally lead him to "curse God and die" (Jb 2:9).

Temptation was the first means employed by Satan to try to dissuade Jesus from his righteous obedience to the Father (Lk 4:1-13). He tempted Jesus to use his power to take care of himself (v.3), to gain his end (i.e., Jesus' reign over the earth) through false worship (vv.6-7), and to put God's care for Jesus to the test (vv.9,10). When every temptation had failed, Luke says that the devil left Jesus but kept looking for other opportunities (v.13).

Jesus warned his disciples that they would undergo a period of severe temptation at the hands of the devil (Lk 22:31). In the parable of the sower and the seed, Jesus says that when the seed of God's word is sown in a man's heart, the devil is close by to see if he can snatch it away through temptation (Mk 4:15). Ephesians 6:16 urges Christians to strongly defend themselves against "the fiery darts of the evil one"—those temptations from the devil which lead men to leave the faith they have received in God.

Many Christians have been lulled into a sleepy attitude toward temptation. In fact, a good many people today wouldn't recognize temptation at all. Yet its insidious and constant character has been one of the major concerns of the holy men and women of God throughout the history of the Church. The Fathers warn of the pressing and insistent nature of satanic temptation:

> For the rest, what else is waged daily in the world but a battle against the devil, but a struggle with continual onsets against his darts and weapons? With avarice, with lewdness, with anger, with ambition, we have a conflict; with the vices of the flesh, with the allurements of the world, we have a continual and stubborn fight. The mind of man besieged and surrounded on all sides by the assault of the devil with difficulty opposes these foes one by one, with difficulty resists them. If avarice is cast to the ground, lust springs up; if lust is put down, ambition takes its place; if ambition is disdained, anger provokes, pride puffs up, drunkenness invites, envy destroys harmony, jealousy severs friendships. You are forced to curse, which the divine law prohibits; you are compelled to swear, which is forbidden.[10]

Cyprian takes pains to point out the relentless nature of satanic temptation. The devil, he says, is a stubborn enemy who makes the most use he can of the world and the flesh in the temptations he hurls at the Christian.

In another book, Cyprian elaborates on this idea:

> For what more fitly or more fully befits our care and solici-
> tude than to prepare the people divinely committed to us
> and the army established in the heavenly camp with con-
> stant exhortations against the weapons and darts of the
> devil? For he cannot be a soldier fit for war who has not
> first been trained in the field, nor will he who seeks to
> obtain the contestant's crown be crowned in the stadium,
> unless he first gives thought to the practice and skill of his
> powers. He is an old adversary and an ancient enemy with
> whom we wage battle. Almost six thousand years are now
> being fulfilled since the devil first attacked man. All kinds
> of tempting and arts and plots for his overthrow has he
> learned by the very practice of a long time. If he finds a
> soldier of Christ unprepared, if untrained, if he does not
> find him vigilant with a solicitous and whole heart, he be-
> sets him in ignorance, he deceives him incautious, he en-
> traps him inexperienced. But if anyone guards the precepts
> of the Lord, and bravely adhering to Christ stands against
> the devil, he must be conquered, since Christ whom we
> confess is invincible.[11]

The purpose of all satanic temptation is to lead men away
from God. In dealing with Christians who are strong in their
faith, the devil attempts to harass and weary them through a
continual barrage of temptations. The Christian is cautioned to
keep alert and to pray lest he fall into temptation (Lk 22:46).
Satan's temptations are as numerous and varied as man's ca-
pacity for sin. He tailors his attacks to fit each individual's own
particular set of weaknesses. To be sure, not every temptation
to sin is a direct result of the influence of Satan or an evil spirit.
Man is provided with enough direct inducements through his
own sinful desires (the flesh), and the inducements afforded by
the world provide him with other powerful temptations. The
indirect cause of all temptation is the devil, but he cannot be
held immediately responsible for every sin. However, if Chris-

tians do not recognize Satan's work where it exists, they will not be able to effectively resist him.

Opposition

Satan and his evil spirits also attack mankind in general and Christians in particular by trying to prevent the preaching of the gospel and the spreading of the kingdom of God. In the lives of individuals, they will attempt to block a person's coming to the Lord or growing in a deeper relationship with the Lord.

In the Acts of the Apostles we see Satan's activity when the magician Elymas opposed the work of Paul and Barnabas:

> When they had gone through the whole island as far as Paphos, they came upon a certain magician, a Jewish false prophet, named Bar-Jesus. He was with the proconsul, Sergius Paulus, a man of intelligence, who summoned Barnabas and Saul and sought to hear the word of God.
>
> But Elymas the magician (for that is the meaning of his name) withstood them, seeking to turn away the proconsul from the faith. But Saul, who is also called Paul, filled with the Holy Spirit, looked intently at him and said, "You son of the devil, you enemy of all righteousness, full of all deceit and villainy, will you not stop making crooked the straight paths of the Lord?" (Acts 13:6-10)

Verse 7 says that Elymas' purpose in opposing Paul's preaching was to prevent the proconsul from becoming a Christian.

In his second letter to the Corinthians, Paul answers a charge made by his enemies that his preaching of the gospel is unclear. Paul answers that his preaching has been an "open statement of the truth." He goes on to say that if the gospel appears veiled to anyone, "It is veiled only to those who are perishing. In their case the god of this world has blinded the minds of the unbelievers, to keep them from seeing the light of the gospel of the glory of Christ, who is the likeness of God" (2 Cor 4:3-4).

"The god of this world," Satan, attempts to darken men's

understanding so that the gospel will seem strange, or silly, or irrelevant. Such is the case in the eighth chapter of John's Gospel in which Jesus notes how Satan was able to manipulate the blindness of the Jews so they cannot receive Jesus. Satan made use of Jesus' claim of his unique relationship with God to stir up the Jews against him (Jn 8). Jesus tells the Jews that they are trying to kill him because they reject the words of his Father and instead believe the words of their own father—the devil (Jn 8:37-38).

Another of Satan's tactics for opposing the preaching of the gospel is seen in Acts 16:16-18:

> As we were going to the place of prayer, we were met by a slave girl who had a spirit of divination and brought her owners much gain by soothsaying. She followed Paul and us, crying, "These men are servants of the Most High God, who proclaim to you the way of salvation."
>
> And this she did for many days. But Paul was annoyed, and turned and said to the spirit, "I charge you in the name of Jesus Christ to come out of her." And it came out that very hour.

Here the evil spirit does not challenge Paul as Elymas did, but rather tries to turn the serious preaching of the gospel into a sideshow. Whether or not the evil spirit was hoping to be left alone by "helping" Paul isn't clear. But Paul refuses to let the testimony of an evil spirit be cause either for accepting or rejecting the gospel. In fact, Paul views it as a definite hinderance and casts it out.

John says that the true spirit of antichrist is opposition to the gospel, and when such opposition is found, the evil one is at the root of it (Jn 3:22).

A brief passage in the book of Daniel sheds further light on the activity of Satan in opposition to God.

> Then he said to me, "Fear not, Daniel, for from the first day that you set your mind to understand and humbled yourself before your God, your words have been heard, and I have

come because of your words. The prince of the kingdom of Persia withstood me twenty-one days; but Michael, one of the chief princes, came to help me, so I left him there with the prince of the kingdom of Persia and came to make you understand what is to befall your people in the latter days. For the vision is for days yet to come." (Dn 10:12-14)

The background to this passage is that Daniel has received a vision. The vision was hard to understand. In fear and confusion, Daniel sought the Lord for the interpretation. God sent the angel Gabriel to bring him both enlightenment (v.14) and courage (v.19), but God's messenger is hindered in his mission by an evil spirit whom Gabriel calls "the prince of the kingdom of Persia." In other words, Satan tries to prevent God from both instructing and encouraging Daniel. It is instructive to note Gabriel's statement that on the very day Daniel began his fast and prayer, God dispatched the angel to help Daniel. However, because of a battle taking place in the spiritual realm, Daniel had to wait a full three weeks for God's enlightenment and encouragement.

This brief glimpse in Daniel of the warfare taking place in the spiritual realm should give all Christians greater faith and patience in their prayers. Often, Christians offer a sincere prayer to God but become discouraged when the answer does not come immediately. The truth is that God is acting, but Satan is often working against it. Satan cannot overcome God's power and will, but the Christian's own lack of faith and perseverance can cut off God's action for him.

The most intensive opposition Satan launched against God's work was to engineer the death of Jesus. When his efforts to tempt Jesus failed (Mt 4:10), Satan sought to remove Jesus from the scene entirely. Indeed, Jesus tells the Jews who are trying to kill him that they are doing what their father the devil tells them to do because "He was a murderer from the beginning" (Jn 8:44). However, while Satan instigated those who killed Jesus, Jesus died of his own free will because the Father wanted him to (Jn 14:30-31). Satan's opposition to God is bounded only by the extent of the power God allows him to wield. In plotting the death of Jesus, Satan thought he was gaining a great victory. In fact, he engineered his own decisive defeat (1 Cor 2:8).

Bondage

Satan's nature is such that he will do anything he can to cut off the full, rich life which God intends for his people to have. Satan uses not only temptation and opposition to keep men from the kingdom, but he also tries to snare mankind into bondage to himself.

In the gospels, the most dramatic encounters between Jesus and the powers of evil occur when Satan has a person in some form of bondage. In Mark 5:1-13, Jesus confronts the awesome bondage of full demonic possession in the man of Gerasene. The man was under such intense demonic possession that the demons named themselves by a corporate entity—Legion (v.9). The possessed man had incredible strength (v.4) and was as much a threat to himself as to anyone else (v.5). The demons had the man in a most wretched condition, but Jesus destroyed the bondage and restored the man to fullness of basic human life.

Another example of satanic bondage by possession is the story of the boy in Matthew 17:14-18. Here the possession takes the form of epilepsy, but Jesus recognizes that the problem is not physical but spiritual. He cures the boy by casting out the demon which had him in bondage.

Jesus also frees a mute from demonic bondage (Mt 9:32) as well as another man whose demonic bondage caused him to be both blind and mute (Mt 12:22). Jesus also asserts that Satan has been responsible for the physical deformity of a woman who had been that way for eighteen years (Lk 13:10).

Besides these physical manifestations of satanic bondage, scripture shows that there also is a directly spiritual form. Paul tells the Galatians that before they came to the Lord, they were in bondage to the "elemental spirits of the universe." (Gal 4:3,8). In 1 Corinthians, Paul says that the heathens are in bondage to idols (1 Cor 12:2).

The Fathers also point out the relationship between idols and demons, especially how demons use idols (false worship) to enslave men to themselves. Justin Martyr writes:

> Moreover, they subsequently subjected the human race to themselves, partly by magic writings, partly by the fear they instilled into them and the punishments they inflicted upon them, and partly by instructing them in the use of sacrifices, incense, and libations, which they really needed after becoming slaves of their lustful passions; and among men they engendered every species of sin.[12]

The modern forms of idolatry—the worship of money, power, self—bring man under satanic bondage just as surely as burning incense at a pagan altar. Augustine points to this when he warns Christians against the ways of the devil.

> He is referring to the Devil where He says, "The prince of this world has been cast out" (Jn 12:31). Not that he has been cast out of the world, as certain heretics suppose, but that he has been cast out of the souls of men who hold fast to the word of God and are not lovers of the world, of which he is the prince. The Devil rules over lovers of temporal goods belonging to this visible world, not because he is lord of this world, but because he is ruler of those covetous desires by which we long for all that passes away. Consequently, those who neglect God, who is eternal, and love what is fleeting and changing, are made subject to him. "For covetousness is the root of all evil, and some in their eagerness to get rich have strayed from the faith and have involved themselves in many troubles" (1 Tm 6:10).
>
> By this covetousness the Devil rules within man and takes possession of his heart. Such are all the lovers of this world.[13]

Satan is not a fair player. His demonic forces will attempt to affect whatever area of life they can. They unceasingly oppose the preaching of the gospel. They try to rob the newly planted seed of the word. They erect obstacles to prevent a person from coming close to God. They will take control of whatever human faculties they are able—physical, spiritual, psychological—in order to rob man of the life God intends for him. Young and old, rich and poor, the powerful and the lowly, male and female are all prey to the satanic onslaught.

FOUR

The Activity of Evil Spirits in Daily Life

In some ways, the above discussion of the modes of satanic activity may seem rather removed from daily life. After all, few Christians have encountered the work of evil in the same dramatic way as Jesus and Paul did. Possession is known mainly from movies such as "The Exorcist." Few Christians have ever seen the real thing. How many congregations have experienced demons crying out through people while the gospel is being preached? Of course, that may have more to do with the poor quality of the preaching than with the absence of evil spirits.

Nevertheless, such dramatic manifestations of evil spiritual activity do take place today, and Satan is becoming more and more open in his work.

However, if we look only for the extreme, the dramatic, or the bizarre, we will miss the ways evil spirits can act upon Christians' lives every day in an unobtrusive and quiet manner. Many of the problems blamed on physical, hormonal, psychological, and environmental factors are actually the work of evil spirits. Perhaps the key ruse of evil spirits is to camouflage themselves. They carry out their work in such a way that people think the havoc they cause is merely the natural working of human life. Only through careful examination and spiritual discernment can the demonic forces get flushed from their "natural" hiding place. To all outward appearances, the infirm woman in Luke 13:10 was suffering from some natural bodily ailment. Those around her were doubtlessly startled when Jesus declared and then proved that the real cause was not physical but demonic. Through his spiritual discernment, Jesus was able to see behind the obvious to the actual cause of the woman's problem. Until Jesus arrived, the demon was perfectly safe and the woman was trapped in a miserable existence, blind to the true cause of her plight.

Today, many Christians suffer in the same way. Many areas of their lives are attacked by evil spirits and are even in bondage to them, but the external manifestations often obscure the real spiritual root of the problem and prevent them from getting the help that they need. In order to get a better grasp on how evil spirits work, let us look at how the three modes of satanic activity mentioned above can manifest themselves in daily lives.

Temptation

Demonic temptation can take place at various levels. The most elementary level is the sharp, one-time enticement which eventually passes, either because it is successfully resisted or eventually given in to. At its most profound level, satanic temptation can result in a bondage to sin which exercises a thorough domination over a person which seems impossible to overcome. Demonic temptation ranges from simple and everyday occurances to bizarre thoughts and expressions. It encompasses everything from "little white lies" to murder and adultery.

The main purpose in demonic temptation is to trap people in sin and keep them off guard. Like military commandos, evil spirits make quick raids into vulnerable areas of life. They look for opportunities to use men's weaknesses to their own advantage. They know how to present the "right" temptation, tailor-made for each person. They gain footholds in people's lives under the cover of the weakness of the flesh. They look for spiritual, physical, emotional, and mental weak points. Keeping close watch on these areas, they look for occasions to strike and inflict whatever damage they can. They will maintain their hold on an area as long as they remain unchallenged.

A woman we know, a wife and mother, recently recounted some troubles she had had. Her story is a good example of the daily, seemingly simple ways evil spirits can tempt us.

Mary woke up one morning feeling emotionally out of sorts. She had no particular reason to feel this way. Things in her life had been going very well for the few days before. Her normal emotional state is pretty level. This particular morning, however, she simply felt a little gloomy and depressed. What's more, her irritability grew worse. Her husband and children didn't receive a very heartfelt "good morning" at the breakfast table. Mary's husband made a couple of attempts to find out what was wrong, but he didn't get much help from Mary. On his way out the door to work, Mary's husband said he would make a special point to pray for her day. Mary quipped, "What makes you think I need special prayer?" Her husband murmured something about being late and beat a hasty retreat.

Later, after everyone was out the door, Mary threw herself into the morning chores. Perhaps it is more accurate to say that Mary *threw* the morning chores: the dishes were decisively placed in the drainer, the bed pillows received more than the usual number of fluffs, and the dog could not quite manage to stay out of her way.

At ten o'clock Mary sat down to pray as she usually did at that time, but she couldn't get herself to concentrate. All manner of distractions kept popping into her mind, things which increased her irritation: the leaky faucet that *he* promised to fix last week, the correspondence she was behind on, the mess in the boys' bedroom. Finally, having now achieved a full-blown state of irritability, Mary turned on the nearest target and snapped, "Well, Lord, just how do you expect me to handle all these things?" (We should add that, in spite of the state she was in at the time, Mary has a very good relationship with the Lord and has a remarkable ability to hear him speak to her.)

Mary's question was rhetorical at best, and she didn't actually expect the Lord to say anything. But he did say something to her. "Mary," he said, "stop and think about how your day has gone so far. You are being harassed by an evil spirit."

What the Lord said opened Mary's eyes. She saw clearly that an evil spirit had capitalized on her emotional state and become the driving force behind her irritability. Mary then repented for her irritability and commanded the evil spirit to leave her alone. She also asked the Lord to help her regain her emotional equilibrium.

Throughout the rest of the day, whenever Mary felt tempted to irritability, she told the evil spirit to leave. As the day wore on, Mary felt less and less inclined to be irritable, and she found that her emotional gloom had lifted. By the time her children returned from school she was her usual self again. She also called her husband at work and told him it was safe to come home for supper.

Evil spirits like to get involved in the little things of the day because they can lead to bigger things. Small irritation can escalate into anger and frustration. Disappointment can become envy and self-pity. These sins can often have their roots in the demonic. Through them, evil spirits can keep Christians' lives off balance, stifle their relationships, and move them toward more opportunities to sin.

Sometimes the demonic root of temptation can be more readily seen. Christians may at times experience temptation to do something which is totally out of character for them. These temptations often seem to come out of nowhere.

Tom, a friend of mine, once told me (Cirner) that periodically he would be severely tempted to have an extramarital affair. I know Tom well, and I and others regard him as one of the best Christian men we have ever met. His temptation didn't make any sense to me because it was so inconsistent with his personality and character.

Nevertheless, the temptation to have an affair periodically attacked Tom. He said that the temptation would come on very suddenly and was usually directed at some specific woman. He had never come even close to yielding to the temptation, and he felt confident that he never would succumb. However, the temptation was very distracting and resisting it consumed a lot of mental and emotional energy. When the temptation began, it usually lasted a week or so and then, just as suddenly as it began, it would stop, leaving Tom very wrung out.

I explained to Tom that I thought this was perhaps a case of satanic temptation and told him how to take authority over it. From that time on, Tom was able to directly confront the demonic force behind the temptation. The temptations became less intense, shorter in duration, and fewer in number. Tom expends much less energy on resisting the temptations since he relies on the authority of the Lord to dispel the evil spirits bothering him.

The kind of temptation Tom was experiencing is not unusual. We can all think of many times in our lives when we felt moved to do something or found ourselves thinking about or desiring something which our basic moral core rebelled at. "That just isn't like me," we say, and we feel shaken to think that the thought or impulse came from us. Often it does not come from us. Its origin can be demonic and its purpose is to keep us off balance, to confuse us, to distract us, to sow seeds of doubt about ourselves and others, and, if possible, to trip us into sin.

When the person does not resist the temptation but gives in to it, it can lead to serious bondage to sin.

At the time I (Cirner) got to know him, Carl was a 23-year-old single man who was living a reasonably mature pattern of Christian life since being baptized in the Holy Spirit three years before. He had graduated from college, gotten established in his professional field, and now wanted to get married. Carl came to get my advice on the matter. During our conversation he brought up a problem: for some years, Carl had had a fairly constant urge to masturbate, an urge he was rarely able to resist. By the time he talked with me, masturbation had become a daily habit. He didn't want to continue in this sinful pattern but he felt unable to do anything about it. He was afraid his habit might be an impediment to marriage.

Carl had tried a couple of different things over the years to handle the temptation. For a while he tried simply resisting through willpower, but this did not work. He weakened quickly each time temptation came. He had also tried distracting himself. When temptation arose, he would try attending to his favorite hobby, take a walk, or do other things to stave off the urge to masturbate. But invariably the temptation proved too strong, and it overpowered all of Carl's attempts at distraction.

In addition to the problem itself, Carl felt terrible about it. His inability to take care of what seemed like a minor problem caused him to lose some of his self-respect. Each time he succumbed to the temptation, he would fall into a sense of guilt and shame which lasted for hours.

I had to admit that Carl had a problem. However, I found it neither new nor unique. I had counselled and prayed with many people, both men and women, who had the same problem with masturbation. Some had more severe cases than Carl, some less. But all experienced the same thing: a compulsive and insistent temptation to masturbate.

After further discussion, I told Carl that I thought he was unable to overcome the problem because the root cause in his case was something other than just ingrained habit or psychological need. I said that my discernment and my experience led me to believe that this problem was at root direct satanic temptation. I explained how evil spirits work on these particular areas in a person's life. We then prayed for a while and I commanded the evil spirit to cease his activity. I also prayed for the Lord to strengthen Carl and give him vigilance against any further attack.

After prayer, I instructed Carl about how to deal with any further temptation toward masturbation. I said he should first of all deal with the urge as the work of an evil spirit. Immediately upon being tempted, he should command the evil spirit to depart. Then I told him to call upon the Lord's strength and exercise his will to resist. Carl left that day feeling like a tremendous burden had been lifted from him.

I see Carl often because I have some responsibility for him in our Christian community. It is clear that his progress in overcoming the masturbation problem has been dramatic. The change began the day we prayed. The frequency of the temptations dropped off significantly right away. When temptations did come, Carl dealt with them the way I suggested. He successfully resisted nearly all the time. Temptation became even less frequent as Carl continued to resist. The last time Carl and I talked, it was clear to me that Carl no longer had a problem. By taking the proper spiritual authority, he had gained mastery over this temptation.

Serious demonic activity of the type that afflicted Carl has some clear characteristics. First, it has an insistent, overwhelming quality. Before Carl realized that his temptation was from a demonic source, none of his methods for dealing with the problem worked. The temptation simply wore him down. The evil spirit played upon a certain psychological mechanism by which Carl finally believed that the only way out of the temptation was to give in to it. Eventually, Carl came to feel resignation each time the temptation began. He knew sooner or later he would give in to the temptation because he saw no other way out.

The demon's insistence and Carl's resignation combined in a second important characteristic of this form of demonic temptation: its compulsive nature. Carl exhibited no control over the problem. When the opportunity (temptation) presented itself, he gave in. In time, he came to the point where he no longer even tried to resist. The act now bypassed his critical faculties altogether and masturbation became something he did habitually without thinking. Yet it was not mere unthinking habit. Carl felt driven to do it. He couldn't see himself not doing it. The whole experience was too overpowering.

Like Carl, some Christians seem to have little or no control over long-standing temptations to sin: sexual immorality, lying, anger, cheating, drunkeness, and foul talk. All of these temptations can be the work of evil spirits. When they are, the problem will not get resolved until the demonic force behind it is unmasked and directly resisted.

Christians will never be completely free of temptations from evil spirits. Some freedom from them can be gained by living a wholesome and stable Christian life, but even a sinless life, wouldn't prevent demonic temptation. Jesus lived a perfectly sinless life, and he was tempted many times by the devil. In fact, it is probably true to say that the more holy a person is,—

that is, the more he is immune to the weakness of his flesh and the allurements of the world—the more the devil and his evil spirits will be directly involved in tempting him.

However, being vulnerable to demonic temptation is not the same as being helpless. As often as temptation is met in whatever form and from whatever source, God gives Christians the grace and authority to overcome it.

Opposition

The form of demonic harassment identified as opposition is concerned with Satan's efforts to keep some good from happening. The "good" can be anything that enables us to be more fruitful and effective in our Christian life. The good can be something that is obviously spiritual, such as preaching the gospel and exercising spiritual gifts. The good can also be something more "ordinary," such as good relationships with other people. As with temptation and personal sin, demonic influence is not always the cause of things going wrong. But when it is the cause, things will not go right until we deal directly with the evil spirits.

For example, evil spirits often try to disrupt the times Christians gather for prayer. I (Cirner) have one vivid memory of such an occasion which took place in the early 1970s. I was the leader of a prayer meeting, usually attended by about two hundred people. It was an open meeting held in the basement of a school. Anyone could come in and join us. We had arranged the chairs in concentric circles; since I was leading the meeting, I sat in the innermost circle. Shortly after we began, a man came into the room and stood at the back observing what was going on. I didn't pay much attention at first because people would often come in out of curiosity, observe for a while, and then either find a place to sit or decide to leave.

As we worshipped the Lord in song and prayer, I suddenly became aware that the man had stopped observing and was causing a disturbance behind the last circle of chairs. He was pacing back and forth, talking to himself, and shaking his head. As he continued to pace, his talking got louder and various parts of his body began to twitch. Those in the prayer meeting sitting closest to him were already paying more attention to him than to the meeting. The rest of the people were quickly getting distracted by the man.

As the leader of the meeting, I knew I should do something about the problem. As I was considering my options, I sensed the Lord saying to me that this was a problem involving an evil spirit. I quickly and silently commanded the evil spirit influencing the man to sit down and be silent. I repeated the command two or three times.

Suddenly, the man stopped talking, walked over to the exit door, sat down on the steps, and fell asleep. He was still asleep when the meeting ended.

The evil spirit's intention in this situation was to disrupt things, to keep people from focusing on the Lord. Many people at the meeting could have easily missed what God wanted to say to them if the disturbance had continued. My silent exercise of spiritual authority got the meeting back on track quickly. The evil spirit was thwarted.

Not all demonic opposition to Christian gatherings is quite so dramatic. Another common form of opposition is for evil spirits to cast a pall of heaviness or lethargy over the meeting. During these times, prayer seems stale, the singing lifeless, and prophecy weak. People are restless. You can almost feel the opposition in the room. We have been at gatherings where the leaders recognized what was happening and commanded the evil spirits harassing them to depart. The change in the tone of the meeting was immediate and obvious. We have also been at gatherings where the leaders knew there was a problem but failed to identify its source. These meetings just plodded along in the most lifeless manner, held together only by the determination of the leaders and the commitment of the rest of the people. When these meetings finally ended, people couldn't wait to leave.

Christians can have this same kind of experience in their own personal prayer time. Some days we find it almost impossible to pray. We can't concentrate; everything we say to the Lord sounds dry and stale. Our spirits seem lifeless.

Sometimes, the source of this problem is our own fault—last night's late-late creature feature or that green pepper and anchovy pizza. But other times, the root cause is direct demonic opposition. Christians can go through life without experiencing what the Lord has for them in prayer and scripture reading because they fail to recognize and deal with the harassment of evil spirits taking place at these times.

Demonic opposition also takes place in our relationships. Evil spirits promote strife and disunity among Christians because these are the opposite of the love and unity which God wants and expects.

Early in our marriage (Cirner), my wife and I noticed that there were times when nothing either of us said could resolve a disagreement. Our most carefully and sensitively chosen words compounded the problem rather than helped it. During one of these times, I said in my mind, "Lord, why isn't this problem getting worked out?" Almost immediately, the thought "evil spirits" came to my mind. I silently commanded the evil spirits to leave, and the whole impasse was resolved within ten minutes.

Later, I told my wife what had happened. We agreed that whenever we found ourselves in one of these situations, we would stop the discussion and cast out any evil spirits at work between us. The results of doing this have been remarkable. The whole tone of our disagreement will change and the problem will be quickly settled.

Evil spirits will also try to prevent people from having a deeper relationship with the Lord. It is common for all kinds of things to go wrong for people just before they are prayed with to be baptized in the Holy Spirit. Fears arise about the experience itself. People get sick. Babysitters cancel out at the last minute. Husbands and wives have the type of argument which leaves both of them cold and hostile. The car breaks down. Doubts about God's love assail the person. Skepticism about the validity of the experience suddenly reasserts itself. In one sense, all of these things can be seen as the ordinary occurrences of life, the normal reactions to something new and unknown. Many times they are just that. However, such circumstances are often the activity of evil spirits attempting to hinder someone's progress toward God.

Christians should expect to encounter demonic opposition as they move toward the Lord. Satan is firm in his determination to keep men and women from knowing the fullness of life with God. Men and women may grow weary and become lax in their striving toward God, but Satan never tires. He presses his advantage when a person weakens. Yet, like the men and women of God who have gone before us, the Christian can look to the Lord for strength and courage to defeat whatever demonic opposition he encounters.

Bondage

Of the three modes of satanic activity, bondage is certainly the most dramatic and distressful. Possession, the most profound form of bondage, is the most terrifying experience a person can have, short of a vision of hell itself. In the state of possession, the demonic is no longer hidden but shows itself plainly in all its power and hate. The true nature of Satan is in view for all to see. No one who has ever seen a possessed person can doubt the absolute, unrelenting, and incorrigible evil present there. One's views of Satan and the demonic can never remain the same after witnessing true possession.

While possession gives the most dramatic view of demonic bondage, lesser forms of bondage still give a clear manifestation of evil.

While praying with a young woman in her twenties for some difficulties she was having, the Lord gave me (Cirner) a very clear word in my mind that she was having trouble with her menstrual period. I asked her about it, and she looked at me totally amazed. "How did you know?" she asked. She said that she had not menstruated in eight years. She had consulted doctors a number of times but they had been unable to help her. She wanted to get married and have a family but wasn't at all sure that she could bear children. She had not been diagnosed as sterile, but she hadn't been reassured either.

As she spoke, I sensed the Holy Spirit saying to me that the problem was demonic bondage. I told the young woman that I believed she was under demonic bondage and that we should pray and command it to leave. We did so, and after asking the Lord to bless her with fertility, I ended the session.

A few weeks later the woman called. She was ecstatic because she had begun her first menstrual period in eight years. She called back some months later to say that not only had she been having her period every month, but that they were more regular than they were before they stopped. She eventually married a fine young man and she has borne two children already.

A man we know, William, was in bondage to fear. He was afraid of almost every situation he would find himself in. William was the ultimate pessimist as he voiced his fears. He was afraid of people and he was afraid to be alone. He was afraid of animals, cars, heights, and storms. He was afraid to join in conversations even when he had something worthwhile to say. Fear was destroying William emotionally and physically.

Several of us who knew William well decided that the time had come to deal with that fear. We were convinced that the root cause was demonic, and we got together with William to pray about it. The prayer session was long and tiring but it was successful. When we broke the hold of the evil spirit on William, he experienced an immediate freedom from fear. Afterwards, he was able to act freely in most of those situations which had previously bound him in fear.

Many people are like William. Some of their emotions are not under their control. Fear is an area of emotional life which evil spirits often bring under bondage. Anger is another common area, one which can be much more destructive to others than fear. Evil spirits can bind men so tightly in anger that it is almost the only response they make to any situation involving even the slightest stress. The destructive force of such anger gets vented on spouse, children, friends, and anyone else who happens to be around. Depression is another common area of bondage. Indeed, any area of one's emotional life can be brought into bondage. When demonic bondage is the root of an emotional problem, no amount of willpower or therapy will bring release. Only the power of the Lord can do it.

Cal was a young man who was about to become a father for the second time. He and his wife were the typical proud parents, and it looked to everyone around them that they had an excellent family life. However, one day Cal came to talk about something he was both puzzled by and afraid of. He had found himself treating his wife and son in a mean and vicious manner. This surprised us because we had known Cal to be a peaceable and controlled individual. The worst thing, Cal explained, was that he was beginning to act just like his father did toward his mother and Cal's brothers and sisters.

Cal's home had not been pleasant. His father was an alcoholic who used to beat his wife and children. The father had a well-paying job, but most of the money went for alcohol and the family just scraped by. Cal was afraid of his father and didn't like him at all. As he grew older, Cal swore to himself that he would never be like his father.

One day, when Cal was in his early teens, he came home and found his father verbally abusing Cal's mother in a terrible manner. When Cal walked into the room, his father turned on him with his verbal abuse and ended by saying, "I know you hate and despise me. But you are no better than me, sonny. You are going to be just like me." Cal said that at that moment, he felt a physical heaviness, as if something had just settled on top of him. A strange sense of foreboding enveloped him. Cal was certain that his father was the last person in the world he wanted to be like, but something inside of him told him he didn't have much choice.

A couple of years later Cal became involved with a teenage Christian group through the influence of his pastor. This brought about a radical change in Cal's life. Over the next five or six years, through the influence and ministry of this Christian group, Cal developed into a fine Christian young man and eventually became a member of the Christian community where he met and married his wife.

His current trouble puzzled Cal because he was sure that his life had been so radically changed over the years that he didn't think it possible for his father's ways to have an effect on him.

Yet, in spite of his new life and contrary to his desires, he was acting like his father in some alarming ways.

We told Cal that what his father had done in his drunkeness and anger had been to open Cal to demonic infiltration. The evil spirit was now trying to exercise his claim on Cal. We prayed and commanded the spirit to depart from Cal. We then closed off any access the evil spirit had as a result of his father's curse. Cal recognized an immediate change in his relationship with his wife and child. By the time their second child was born, the problem was completely gone.

The curse of a parent, scripture says, can have devastating effects on a child's life (Sir 3:9). Cal's father left him completely vulnerable to demonic incursion as a result of his rash speech. Many times parents unknowingly subject their children to some form of demonic bondage through what they say and do. Parents are meant to provide spiritual protection and blessing for their children, yet many parents fail to grasp that food, clothing, shelter, and education, necessary as they are, do not deal with a child's spiritual needs. Parental curses, deliberately or ignorantly invoked, parental involvement with the occult, astrology, spiritism, parental bondage to drugs, in short, any form of parental bondage to evil spirits or serious abnegation of responsibility can expose their children to evil spirits. Sad to say, Cal's experience is not an uncommon one.

Speech is another area where evil spirits can hold Christians in bondage. Many years ago, while praying with a group of people to be baptized in the Holy Spirit, I (Cirner) encountered a woman who was having tremendous difficulty praying in tongues. At first I suspected that she had the common difficulty of embarrassment. I was about to encourage her to be patient and to wait until she was alone before God to yield herself to the gift. But something checked this impulse. I sought the Lord for a moment, and thought he was telling me that the woman had a very serious problem with foul talk. In fact, she was in such bondage to it that she was not able to freely exercise her mouth to praise and worship God.

I told the woman what I thought. I said that she would need to repent and have that demonic bondage broken before she could pray in tongues. The woman readily admitted the problem, but said she wasn't ready to give it up. She didn't see anything wrong with her foul talk. She left, saying that if she ever changed her mind she would come back. I haven't seen her since.

Like this woman, many people are reluctant to break with the bondage they are in. Sometimes they do not recognize bondage as bondage. Other times, they are afraid to do what's necessary to be free from it. Sometimes, bondage will affect a person's will; a person may recognize his or her peril, but be unable alone to combat the strength of the evil spirit.

Other qualities of the mind can also be brought into demonic bondage. Strange or bizarre daydreaming, thoughts, or desires; impulsive or undisciplined thinking; loss of contact with reality are not always the product of just human factors. The ravings of the psychotic might actually be the ravings of the possessed. A neurotic's compulsive dwelling on death may in reality be the web of demonic bondage. An undisciplined mind is not always the sign of true "genius." An inability to concentrate for any length of time cannot always be blamed on tension and stress.

The mind is one of the key channels between man and God. When Satan controls the mind, he has a strategic advantage over the direction of a person's life. God's word in scripture, prophecy, the sacraments, and spiritual writings often fails to affect a person's life because it falls not on the fertile soil of a mind under self-control, but on the impenetrable rock of a mind in bondage. At best, a mind under demonic bondage receives only a small portion of the richness of God's word.

Evil spirits can also bring people into bondage through control over some aspect of their physical life. The young woman with menstrual problems was an example of such bondage. We have also seen demonic bondage working in allergies, disease, epilepsy, terminal illnesses, arthritis, and skin problems.

The demonic can infiltrate almost every area of human life. The effects of the demonic can be debilitating and of long-term duration, robbing Christian men and women of their rightful share of God's goodness here and now. The grim picture of demonic activity portrayed here should sober God's people, but not frighten them. They are not helpless in the face of the onslaughts of evil spirits. Let us consider the weapons God has given his people to engage in spiritual warfare.

FIVE

Defeating the Power of Satan

A t the end of the Gospel of Mark, Jesus speaks these words to his disciples just before he ascended to his Father:

> Go into all the world and preach the gospel to the whole creation. He who believes and is baptized will be saved; but he who does not believe will be condemned. And these signs will accompany those who believe: in my name they will cast out demons; they will speak in new tongues; they will pick up serpents, and if they drink any deadly thing, it will not hurt them; they will lay their hands on the sick, and they will recover. (Mk 16:15-18)

Luke's Gospel gives the report of the seventy disciples returning after their first preaching venture: "Lord, even the demons are subject to us in your name." Jesus replies:

> I saw Satan fall like lightning from heaven. Behold, I have given you authority to tread upon serpents and scorpions, and over all the power of the enemy; and nothing shall hurt you. (Lk 10:17-19)

Jesus knew that his disciples would encounter the powers of hell in the same way that he had. He knew that the realm of evil presented a far greater challenge to his disciples than the Roman Empire and its armies. He knew that the later generations of disciples—generation after generation until the end of time—would also face the same stark reality, as Satan and his legions attempted to thwart the plan of God for the world.

Therefore, Jesus equips those who follow him for battle. He makes all those who believe in him his brothers and sisters, sons and daughters of the Father. He gives them his Holy Spirit, which changes their very nature. They share in the very life of God. Those who believe are no longer enslaved to the things of this world, but have been set free to enjoy the life of God as his children. Those who believe are "where Christ is, seated at the right hand of God" (Col 3:1), and have received the power of the Holy Spirit to carry on Christ's mission in the world. Without the power of God, man is helpless before the satanic forces.

Christians carry on spiritual warfare from this perspective. Power and victory and authority belong to the Lord, and he has given it to his disciples.

Cyril of Jerusalem says that the Christian's position in relation to evil is radically different after receiving the power of the Holy Spirit:

> When you have received the grace [of baptism], there will be given you thereafter the power to wrestle against the adverse powers. For just as Jesus, after his baptism endured forty days temptation (and that not because he could not surmount it before baptism, but because he willed to accomplish all things in order and sequence), so you, who, prior to baptism, dare not engage the adversaries in strife, when you receive the grace [of baptism] and thenceforth take courage, may then fight with the arms of righteousness, and, if you will, preach the gospel.[14]

Weapons Against Evil Spirits

How does the power of the Holy Spirit within Christians overcome evil spirits? The scriptures and the early Fathers distinguish two principal means of dealing with the work of the devil.

The first means is a straightforward command to Satan and evil spirits to leave a person or a situation. After the temptations in the desert, Jesus commanded the devil to depart from him (Mt 4:10). Jesus ordered the epileptic spirit to leave the boy (Mk 10:25), and he dealt with the Legion through a word of command (Mk 5:8). When Jesus confronted Satan and evil spirits, he dealt with them as someone who was greater and more powerful. He simply ordered Satan to leave.

Jesus referred to this same power and authority when he told his disciples to cast out demons in his name (Mk 16:17). The early Church recognized that the name of Jesus the Christ was an authority that evil spirits could not resist. Paul, for example, cast out a spirit of divination "in the name of Jesus Christ" (Acts 16:18).

The Christians in the first few centuries of the Church used the word of command in the name of the Lord Jesus to exorcise those under demonic bondage. The following quotes, from the writings of Justin Martyr and Irenaeus, illustrate this:

> For many demoniacs throughout the entire world, and even in your own city, were exorcised by many of our Christians in the name of Jesus Christ, who was crucified under Pontius Pilate; and our men cured them, and they still cure others by rendering helpless and dispelling the demons who had taken possession of these men, even when they could not be cured by all the other exorcists, and exploiters of incantations and drugs.[15]

> Through the invocation of the name of Jesus Christ, crucified under Pontius Pilate, Satan is cast out from men, and wherever anyone shall call upon Him, invoking Him, of those who believe in Him and do His will, He comes and stands close by, accomplishing the petitions of those who invoke Him with a pure heart.[16]

In the fourth century, Athanasius said that the sign of the cross—the symbol of the defeat of demonic powers at the hands of Jesus—invokes his authority and commands demons to leave:

> And while in times past demons, occupying springs or rivers or trees or stones, cheated men by deceptive appearances and imposed upon the credulous by their juggleries, now, after the divine coming of the Word, an end is put to their deceptions. For by the sign of the cross, a man but using it, their wiles are put to flight.[17]

This teaching of scripture and the early Church is preserved today in the prayers of exorcism found in both the Roman Ritual and the Anglican Book of Common Prayer. When Christians directly encounter Satan and his evil spirits, they put them to flight through a word of command invoked in the name of the Lord Jesus Christ.

The second means of dealing with demonic spirits is by making oneself less vulnerable to them. Christians often invite demonic attack by allowing themselves to be in unprotected positions. Without the proper defenses, Christians become easy prey for the devices of evil spirits.

Sin places Christians on precarious ground. By its very nature, sin cuts a man off from the life of God and escorts him into the camp of the enemy. Satan knows about the effects of sin much more clearly than man does. That is why his forces are constantly vigilant, looking for opportunities to tempt man to sin. John says that it is the devil's nature to sin and that whoever sins partakes of the devil's own nature (1 Jn 3:8). Through sin, the Christian gives the devil access to his life. Paul warns Christians not to give the devil an opportunity in their lives by sinning (Eph 4:27). Augustine makes the point more fully:

> Many people, however, ask this question: "How can we overcome the Devil, since we do not see him?" The answer is that we have a Master who has deigned to show us how invisible foes are conquered, for the Apostle said of Him: "Freeing Himself of His body, He made an example of the

principalities and powers, confidently triumphing over them within Himself" (Col 2:15). Consequently, when invisible and sinful desires are overcome, we then overcome the unseen power of our enemy. Hence, by overcoming within ourselves the inordinate love for things temporal, we are necessarily, within ourselves, overcoming him who rules within man by these sinful desires. For, at the time when it was said of the Devil: "Thou shalt eat earth," it was said to the sinner: "Thou art earth, and into earth shalt thou go" (Gen 3:14,19).

What is here implied is that the sinner has been handed over as food for the Devil. And so, if we would not be eaten by the Serpent, we should not become earth. Just as the food our body assimilates becomes a part of us, so by a bad life of wickedness, pride, and ungodliness do we become ourselves one with the Devil. That is to say, we become like the Devil, and just as our body is subject to us, so we are made subject to him. This is the meaning of the expression, "To be eaten by the serpent." Hence, all who fear the fire prepared for the Devil and his angels should take means to overcome the Devil within themselves. For we win an interior victory over the adversaries who assail us from without by conquering the evil desires by which those adversaries hold sway over us. And those whom they find like themselves they drag along with them unto punishment.[18]

Living life as free as possible from sin is surely a powerful deterrent to demonic influence, but avoiding sin is only the minimum. The Christian must also be living his whole life for God in the power of the Spirit. In a famous passage, Paul uses the phrase "the armor of God" to describe the activities involved in spiritual warfare:

Therefore take the whole armor of God, that you may be able to withstand in the evil day, and having done all, to stand. Stand therefore, having girded your loins with truth, and having put on the breastplate of righteousness, and having shod your feet with the equipment of the gospel of peace; above all taking the shield of faith, with which you can quench all the flaming darts of the evil one. And take the helmet of salvation, and the sword of the Spirit, which is the word of God. Pray at all times in the Spirit, with all prayer and supplication. (Eph 6:13-18a)

Paul is saying that the Christian's protection against the attacks of the devil consists not only of righteous living (avoiding sin) but also of positive action such as preaching the gospel, living in the truth of God, having faith in his word, praying and interceding for others, speaking and hearing the word of God, and having a firm conviction of his position in God.

The scriptures contain much more teaching about how to live in God and in peace with one another than teaching about how to discern and cast out evil spirits. The reason, as Paul explains, is that living a righteous and holy life before God in unity with Christian brothers and sisters, is the best weapon. Such a life eliminates many of the opportunities evil spirits have to attack Christians. Living a dynamic Christian life surrounds the Christian with a strong, protective "armor" which evil spirits have a very difficult time penetrating.

In the war with Satan, the Christian has two main weapons, one offensive and the other defensive. The offense is the word of command in the name of the Lord Jesus; the defensive is a dynamic Christian life. Let's see how both of these weapons should concretely be part of the Christian's life.

A Dynamic Christian Life

Five elements should be present in a dynamic Christian life. Let us consider each of them briefly.

Daily Prayer and Scripture Reading

The backbone of the Christian life is time spent with God. The time spent in prayer and scripture strengthens a Christian's relationship with the Lord. It provides an opportunity for God to speak to the Christian and teach him about God himself, God's thoughts, God's ways, and God's plan.

The Lord should be given quality time, not just the time left over from work, hobbies, television, the newspaper, and the other things which a person might prefer to do. The Christian who lacks a regular and consistent time with the Lord will soon find his once-fervent Christian life begin to go stale. The man or woman who does not spend regular time with the Lord is exposed to the temptation to grow even more lax.

Participation in a Christian Group

The Christian life is not meant to be lived alone by isolated individuals. Most Christians realize this, yet the majority of Christian parishes and congregations offer little by way of committed, corporate fellowship among the members. Much of the teaching in the New Testament was written to communities and presupposes a community way of life for those to whom the writings were addressed. Yet Christian communities of the New Testament kind do not exist in most portions of the Church.

To receive the regular support and encouragement they need, Christian men and women should get involved with a group of people who are committed to share their lives together in a significant way, who have a lasting commitment to one another based on the common goal of living in the kingdom of God. Usually the group will meet together regularly to pray and build relationships, to seek the Lord together, and to pray for each other. Personal relationships are another important aspect of such groups and the commitment to love, peace, and unity should be foremost.

Teaching on Christian Living and Truth

The Christian should immerse himself in solid foundational teaching on the Christian life. Ignorance of the foundations of the gospel message and the truths of the Christian life is a valuable ally of evil spirits. By seeking out sound, orthodox Christian teaching, the Christian is able to guard his mind against slick and novel ideas which pose as Christian truth but ultimately lead to dead ends or to thinking which is fuzzy, inconsistent, and often inimical to Christianity.

Christians should make use of the Church Fathers and sound teachers, preachers, and scripture scholars to keep their knowledge of the truth growing in the right way.

Sacramental Life

Christians from sacramental traditions should make frequent use of the sacraments in accordance with their particular tradition. The Eucharist especially is attested to be a source of life and strength for the Christian.

Service to Others

Caring for others is a key element in the Christian's life. Preaching the gospel to those who need to hear it pushes back the frontiers of the kingdom of darkness and furthers the kingdom of God. Providing people with such basic necessities of life as food, clothing, and shelter makes the Christian an active participant in God's provident care for the world.

Christians do not need to go very far from home to encounter needs. We should serve the fatherless family down the street, the elderly couple next door, and members of our own community or prayer group who may be in material or financial need.

The elements of a dynamic Christian life have balance. Christians should be concerned both for their own life with the Lord and for the needs of others. The balance is important. An over-emphasis on the former leads to self-concern and over-spiritualism. An over-emphasis on the latter cuts a person off from the source of the only true help there is for those in need.

The Word of Command

The word of command addressed to evil spirits is simple and direct. Its purpose is to drive evil spirits from the situation at hand. Its most common form is, "You evil spirit, I command you in the name of the Lord Jesus to leave."

The word of command was seen in most of the examples given earlier and will be further illustrated in the next section of the book.

The word of command directed at an evil spirit is not simply a formula. There is nothing magical or automatic about it. Note what happened to Sceva's sons who thought it was merely a formula (Acts 19). It is intended to be a statement of faith and authority. It affirms the Christian's faith in the redemptive act of the Lord Jesus who freed mankind from slavery to the demonic. And it proclaims the source of the authority now being exercised over the evil spirit.

There is, of course, the need for caution. The Christian is not at liberty to indiscriminately command evil spirits to leave people, places, and situations. The next section details the pastoral context within which deliverance should take place.

SIX

What Is Deliverance?

Deliverance can take place in four ways. In order to define deliverance, we will consider each of the ways Christians can deal with the activity of evil spirits.

Types of Deliverance

Personal or Self-Deliverance

It is important to understand that deliverance ministry is not always necessary in order to be freed from the bondage of evil spirits. In fact, most bondage is broken by the individual himself apart from a special ministry session. Usually this happens in two ways:

1. Significant growth in personal holiness is sufficient in itself to create a spiritual climate which drives away evil spirits. This is especially true when the growth in holiness occurs in the area bound by the evil spirits. For instance, a married man may attack bondage in the area of masturbation by making a new commitment to be faithful to his wife and to be chaste. If this commitment is supported by a general growth in prayer and greater zeal in Christian living, the bondage may be broken.

2. If, however, bondage persists, the person might minister to himself through what is called self-deliverance, commanding the spirits to leave in the name of Jesus: "In the name of Jesus,

I command you, spirit of [lust, anger, etc.] to get out of my life and to stay out."

Such an action of self-deliverance can be very effective and should be employed by all Christians. It is especially necessary when a person has been freed from evil spirits in a particular area but has subsequently fallen back into a sin which was connected with the original bondage. Thus, someone who had been freed from bondage to a spirit of hate, for example, might later fall back into a sin of hate. Such a person should repent and receive forgiveness, but should also command any spirit of hate to depart in the name of Jesus. This self-deliverance is good protection against evil spirits again establishing a hold in the person's life. It seems to be a rule that a person is more likely to be affected by an evil spirit which once had a hold in his life than he is by one which never had him in bondage.

While Christians should expect to be freed from the bondage of evil spirits through growth in holiness and through self-deliverance, they should also be ready to submit to the deliverance ministry of others when necessary.

Fraternal Deliverance

God will often work through other Christian brothers and sisters to deliver someone from the work of evil spirits. Men and women who have committed themselves to be brothers and sisters in the Lord take on a care for one another which extends to all areas of life. There are times when the type of demonic harassment a person is undergoing leaves the person with little faith or conviction that he can deal with the problem by himself. This is when the person turns to his brothers and sisters for their help to cast away the evil spirit and his influence. People who are in committed relationships can help each other in this way because of the basic love and commitment that exists among them.

Pastoral Deliverance

When a person has pastoral responsibility for other people, the Lord gives that person the gifts and authority to deal with deeper and more complex workings of evil spirits. Parents, for example, have received the necessary authority to protect their children and home from demonic activity. In fact, if more Christian parents realized the extent to which evil spirits were attacking their children and home and assumed their rightful authority over the situation, Christian family life would be in much better condition. Later chapters will detail our pastoral care approach to deliverance.

The Special Ministry

God has given to some people special gifts of discernment, revelation, and authority to overcome Satan and evil spirits at their most profound levels of activity. Special ecclesiastically appointed exorcists are empowered to free people from the most serious forms of possession. They are able to bring deliverance from strong, complex, and subtle forms of demonic bondage, bondage which the other three types of deliverance could not deal with.

Deliverance from the work of evil spirits often needs to proceed progressively. This, in fact, has been our experience in the deliverance ministry. Because of the nature of a problem or the person's inability to handle it, it is often necessary to begin to deal with evil spiritual activity on an elementary level. This can often be done by the individual personally, or with the fraternal support of brothers and sisters. This will bring the person a certain amount of freedom and give him some time to stabilize his defenses. Later, as the person grows in strength and faith, deliverance can proceed to a deeper level. This usually requires wise pastoral guidance. The process continues until the person and those caring for him reach the core of the problem and bring about full and final freedom.

Deliverance and Exorcism

Crucial to the approach of this book is the distinction of deliverance, also known as simple exorcism, from solemn exorcism. We are supporting a ministry which can be executed by laypeople or Catholic clergy without any special permission of local ordinaries or other Church authorities. There should always be a general understanding and approval by the bishop for such ministry in the jurisdiction of his diocese, but no particular authorization is needed in the case of deliverance/simple exorcism.

Only priests specifically authorized by the local ordinary may be involved in solemn exorcism; a discussion of such situations is beyond the scope of this book.

Many people who are unfamiliar with the deliverance ministry confuse it with solemn exorcism and therefore question whether it can be performed by laypersons or clergy without specific authorization. For these reasons it is worthwhile to develop the authority for our position and practice.

Solemn exorcism is for the purpose of driving out the devil from a possessed person. The Church requires that such exorcism be public, that is, that it be done in the name of and with the authority of the Church.[19] Canon Law requires that only a priest specifically approved by the local bishop can engage in public exorcism; therefore only such an authorized priest is approved for solemn exorcism.[20]

Simple exorcism, however, is for the purpose of curbing the devil's power and can be executed through private exorcism, which means the exorcist acts in his own name. H. Noldin, a recognized moral theologian, writes: "Private exorcism which truly is not sacramental can be executed by all the faithful . . . The effectiveness of this exorcism is not derived from the authority or prayers of the Church, nor is it done with the name of the Church, but in virtue of the name of God and Jesus Christ."[21]

St. Alphonsus Ligouri supports this position in *Praxis Confessarii*, para. 113, where he discusses the spirit of fornication, teaching that when such a spirit infests a person he will not be able to resist temptations. St. Alphonsus urges confessors, before doing anything else, to pronounce an exorcism against the demon, at least privately, in this manner: "I, as a minister of God, command you, unclean spirit, to depart from this creature of God."[22]

Further, Aldolphe Tanquery, author of the basic American seminary text on spirituality, *The Spiritual Life*, writes:

> If it is morally certain or highly probable that there is diaboli-cal obsession, the spiritual director may make use, in pri-vate, of the exorcisms contained in the Roman Ritual or of some shorter formulas. Should he determine to do so, he should not tell the penitent beforehand if he has reason to fear that it would only worry and excite him; it will suffice to say that he is going to recite over him some prayer approved by the Church. Solemn exorcism may not be employed with-out the permission of the Ordinary and then only with the precautions which he shall indicate when treating of possession.[23]

Tanquery states further in the chapter:

> However, priests may perform private exorcisms employing some prayers of the Church or other formulas. Even lay persons may recite such prayers but not in the name of the Church.[24]

Noldin urges priests to use simple exorcism:

> It is much to be desired that ministers of the Church should perform simple exorcism more frequently, remembering the words of the Lord: "In my name they shall cast out de-mons," especially over those who are vexed by vehement temptations and upon penitents who are experiencing diffi-culties in eliciting sorrow and amendment from sin or sincer-ity in manifesting sins. They should use this or a simpler formula: "In the name of Jesus Christ I command you un-clean spirit to leave this creature of God."[25]

Again this position is supported by moralists McHugh and Callan in their standard text on moral theology:

> As to their manner, exorcisms are also of two kinds, the solemn and the private. The former are made in the name of

the Church in the manner prescribed by the Ritual and their administration is reserved to clerics who have a special and express permission from the Ordinary (Canon 1151). The latter kind may even be made by members of the laity, and we read that certain saints like St. Anthony of the Desert and St. Catherine of Siena, had great power over evil spirits. It is recommended that priests frequently use private exorcisms at least secretely for persons who are vexed by temptations or scruples and for which they may use the form: "In the name of Jesus Christ, unholy spirit, I command you to depart from this creature of God."[26]

Finally, this position that private exorcism may be ministered by the laity is further supported by Prummer who writes: "Not only clerics who have the power of orders but also the laity are able to use exorcism in a private and separate or secret manner."[27]

It is clear from the above authorities as well as other sources which they cite that the laity may perform simple exorcisms which we have preferred to call by the more common term, "deliverance."

It is also clear that priests should regularly exercise this deliverance ministry in the sacrament of reconciliation. Whenever a priest discerns the presence of evil spirits in the penitent, he should make a decision on the most pastorally effective procedure. Sometimes he will suggest a separate deliverance ministry session. He should do this when there is sufficient need and the conditions outlined in Chapter Seven are met.

Sometimes he will invite the penitent to rebuke the evil spirit, and he will join with the penitent in the command. The priest will only do this if he knows the penitent to be sufficiently grounded in principles of spiritual warfare. Frequently, he will have recourse to the procedure referred to in the above citations and silently rebuke and cast out the evil spirit.

It is not our intention in this book to deal with exorcism. This book concentrates on a pastoral approach to deliverance. Our purpose is to give basic teaching and guidance about deliverance in the normal situations of Christian living. We do not deal with exorcism of possessed people. Neither do we deal with the relatively small number of cases of unusually dramatic manifestations of spiritual bondage which do not involve possession.

Solemn exorcism should be used only in cases of possession. These are cases where Satan is able to take over the personality of the affected person and is able to frustrate the person's exercise of free will. The question arises then, when do we stop a deliverance because the person is possessed? The local bishop makes the final determination in cases of possession, so our answer must be a limited one. We may reach the conclusion that a person's condition is beyond the approach outlined here. This does not mean that the person is possessed, but only that possession is a possible reason why this approach is inappropriate.

If a person has sufficient control over himself to repent, renounce spirits, and command them to leave, we can take the initiative and use deliverance successfully. If the person cannot do this because he cannot say the words, goes into a trance, or gives way to a new personality, then we would stop deliverance and pursue other remedies. We have referred such cases for psychological testing, additional spiritual discernment, and, when they persist in this condition, ultimately to the local bishop for his decision regarding solemn exorcism.[28]

There are many manifestations of Satan and demons which are not treated in this book. Some of these are detailed in the Roman Ritual chapter on Exorcism. Others do not constitute necessary knowledge for the normal situations treated here.

SEVEN

Conducting the
Deliverance Ministry

The pastoral model which we have found most effective in conducting the deliverance ministry will be introduced here with three case studies. The pastoral model was used in all three cases. They illustrate our recommended approach and set the stage for the discussion of this approach later in the chapter.

Case Studies

A Married Woman

I had been listening to Jennifer speak about her life. Her husband had commented occasionally, and I had asked a few questions. Now after thirty minutes she had finished her account. As Jennifer shifted in her chair and leaned back, I (Fr. Scanlan) summarized the discussion. My summary went something like this. "It seems," I said, "that you concluded that you needed to succeed on your own and keep everyone else out of your life since no one was to be trusted. You saw your parents as only caring about your achievements and not about you. You saw your older sister and brother as receiving all the affection and affirmation and therefore as your rivals. This set a pattern in your life in which you always disguised your inner self and put on a front of contentment and peace while inside you were gripped by fears of failure and being abandoned. This was reinforced by your experiences in school when you were mocked and generally made fun of whenever you broke down crying. Now in your marriage you have increasingly struggled with a paralyzing fear that your husband may leave you and that your friends will someday discover who you really are and move away from you. The more your fear grows the more activities you engage in to win the love and respect of your family and friends."

Jennifer, an apparently happily married woman with a family, was seeking ministry for deliverance. Present were Jennifer, her husband, and myself, her husband's pastor. I had suggested the session after a meeting with them, not because of any crisis in Jennifer's life or in the family, but because of the situation acknowledged by all of us that Jennifer needed greater freedom and peace in her life and that there should be a more supportive union between Jennifer and her husband.

The husband had aided the session by supplying background information to his wife's comments, by reminding her of important events and by asking leading questions. The husband himself had received ministry for deliverance the preceding month. He understood the importance of the session and the material which would be most useful.

I had begun the session with prayer. Following the prayer I asked, "Jennifer, I want you to tell me what major blocks exist in your life. Where do you experience continual hurt and what concerns preoccupy your thoughts?" She then developed her story in about thirty minutes and I summarized it to her satisfaction. I then proposed how we would pray and she and her husband agreed. First, we would place ourselves under the authority and protection of the Lord Jesus Christ. Then, in the name of Jesus, we would take authority over Satan and the kingdom of evil. Finally, I would lead Jennifer in addressing the specific areas which were bound up in her life.

After the preliminary prayers I asked Jennifer whether she was ready to forgive those who wronged her. She said, "Yes, I forgive my mother, my father, my brother and sister, and my companions who made fun of me." She then specifically forgave each person, and mentioned the wrong she believed they had done. I then led her to repent of sins and to ask God for the gift of faith. She repented and asked for faith. I then asked her to commit herself to trust those who love and care for her. She stated, "I *decide* now to trust all those who love me and care for my life, and I ask the Lord to give me the grace I need to live out this decision to trust."

I asked Jennifer to renounce the spirit of fear and to command it to leave her life. She responded, "I renounce all false fear and in the name of Jesus I cast it out of my life." Jennifer's husband and I entered into the prayer of authority with her and commanded the spirit of fear to leave. I then asked her to renounce and command the spirit of false independence to depart from her life. She repeated the same process and then repeated it again for the spirit of rebellion. After that there was a period of silence; then Jennifer said, "I feel free; there is real peace in me."

At this point I suggested we pray for healing of relationships. Jennifer stated that she had struggled to love her family but, with the exception of her father, she had never succeeded. We began with Jennifer's relationship with the Lord. She repented for not trusting him and she renewed her commitment to him as Lord and Savior. She was able to easily picture Jesus with his arms outstretched to her; as we prayed, she envisioned herself going to him and being held by him. Then she pictured in turn her father, mother, brother, and sister going to Jesus and being embraced by him. Then she pictured Jesus bringing her family to her and slowly leading them to embrace one another.

There was a quiet but visible change in Jennifer as she opened her heart to that love. I explained that the picture process was just an instrument to help her yield herself and to cooperate with the power of the Holy Spirit and the graces God was giving her. We prayed that Jennifer would be strengthened in all areas of trust.

The three of us then talked about the future. How was Jennifer to break from her old habits? Her husband agreed to help her in many ways, especially by setting aside a few minutes each evening to talk about their lives and to review how she was doing in the areas of trust and fear. They both agreed to an extended time once a week. She mentioned some ways she thought he had left her alone to make major decisions and handle certain responsibilities. Her husband agreed that that was a problem. He agreed not to do that again, and asked her to tell him in their evening sharing time whenever she thought he was not taking his rightful responsibility. I counselled Jennifer on how to pray and how to use scripture to build up her life. We then prayed together for God's blessings and protection for the couple and their family.

At the end of the session I gave them a card which pinpointed what we had done. The card listed four categories:

Root Problem: Experience of being abandoned and having to survive through willpower achievements.
Response: Fear and rebellion

Bondage:
Primary: Spirit of fear
Secondary: False independence, rebellion
Manifestation: False front, compulsion to work, unwillingness to reveal weakness or seek help, and general fatigue.

Ministry: Repentance; forgiveness of family; deliverance from fear, false independence, rebellion; inner healing of relationships with Lord and family.

Pastoral direction: Concentrate in prayer on Jesus being your Savior and the need to see yourself as saved and forgiven. Put scripture passages such as these on cards: "Fear is useless, what is needed is trust;" "Do not live in fear, little flock. It has pleased your Father to give you the kingdom;" and, "Faith is confident assurance concerning what we hope for and conviction about things we do not see." Read the cards when tempted to fear and lack of trust. Schedule nightly sharing and a weekly discussion between husband and wife to reinforce decisions and review progress.

A Businessman

During the following week there were two other deliverance sessions. The first involved a seemingly successful business-man who exhibited constant restlessness. Two of us met with him and the session was similar to the one we had had with Jennifer. We reviewed his history of successes and failures in business, parish, and family life. (His account revealed strong ambition, ongoing frustration, and long-term anger.) At the end of the session, the person ministering with me made notes and summarized them on a card.

Root Problem: Sense of hopelessness bordering on despair coming from a series of apparent failures and the current experience of being trapped.
Response: Expecting things to get worse and new ventures to fail; looking for the worst to happen.

Bondage:
Primary: Despair .
Secondary: False ambition

Ministry: Repentance for sins against hope and for striving to reach the top of the business world, regardless of God's plan for his life. Deliverance from despair, pessimism, self-pity, false ambition, and resentment. Inner healing prayer for re-lationships with those who were instrumental in business failures and prayer for healing of the memories of two crisis events in past life. Prayer for gift of hope.

Pastoral Direction: Daily prayer for hope. Scripture readings on the Lord's coming and the glory promised to his faithful servants. Immediately dismiss any thoughts dealing with past wrongs and failures. Regular sharing of struggle with a group of men. Daily recommitment to the Lord's plan, what-ever it is, for his life.

A Christian Leader

The second ministry session involved a man who was an effective leader, a good teacher of the Christian life, who suffered from severe anxiety. He was strong enough to give leadership to others, but he periodically gave way to an over-whelming sense of anxiety. After a long session in which two others in pastoral authority participated, I wrote on the card:

Root Problem: Parental formation demanding perfection in all things, reinforcement in religious training.
Response: Imposing expectations on self to achieve perfection, and constant fear of falling short of expectations.

Bondage: Self perfectionism
Manifestation: Anxiety concerning correct clothes, order of furniture, completing sufficient work in a day, not disappointing others.

Ministry: Repentance: Decision to accept self as sinful, frequently failing, imperfect in all things. Sought forgiveness of co-opting role as savior and made decision to rely on God's mercy. Deliverance from perfectionist spirit, fear of rejection. Inner healing: resentment against mother and excessive fear of God.

Pastoral direction: Recall decisions made and resist any temptations to evaluate or reopen decisions made. Whenever anxiety emerges in a new area, write down your expectations for the situation and then write down the lesser expectations which are consistent with your limited and fallible nature. Then make the best decision you can in light of God's grace and to act on the decision. Approach all such situations with a commitment to be decisive. List scripture passages which exhort decisiveness over fearfulness and use these scriptures daily.

I regularly meet with this man, and it is clear to me that our ministry session was a major breakthrough in his life. He has grown in peace, confidence, and the ability to adjust to sudden changes in his schedule.

The foregoing accounts illustrate the approach to deliverance we have followed for the past few years. They relate three of the many similar sessions in which we have employed the ministry of deliverance to free a person for continued growth toward Christian maturity. The sessions center on deliverance but include prayer and guidance. Most importantly, the session is preceded by many months of pastoral care in which there have been prayer sessions, teaching, counseling, and guidance. Therefore, the deliverance ministry should be considered as one element in a process of pastoral care. Finally, the particular format used in the above cases is not essential as long as the key elements described are included.

A Pastoral Care Approach to Deliverance

We believe the total pastoral care approach to deliverance should be taken whenever possible. Christian communities and parishes have the basic framework in which this pastoral care can be developed. Communities and parishes can develop a pastoral care system whereby individual members can commit their lives to Jesus as Savior and Lord and receive the release of the power of the Holy Spirit and grow to full Christian maturity.

In the process of pastoring people to maturity in the Lord, one or more areas of blockage or bondage will often be uncovered. Individuals will experience an inability to overcome a fear, anxiety, resentment, habitual sin, or compulsion, even though their minds understand clearly that such conduct is not right, their heart's desire is to do what is right, and their wills have decided to act righteously. In other words, people will have these obstacles even though their general spiritual state is such that they should be receiving sufficient grace to enable them to act righteously. The work of evil spirits is most clearly discerned in such circumstances. They are areas of darkness marring a life lived in the light. The deliverance ministry can be most effective in such circumstances. Not only can the person be freed of the bondage, but the basic Christian support system of pastoral care already present is able to secure the person's new freedom and prevent a relapse into sin and bondage.

Other Approaches

Other approaches to deliverance tend to isolate one aspect of the pastoral care approach. Many of them use different people at different times for specialized ministries. We do not believe that these approaches work as well as ones which integrate deliverance into a system of pastoral care. The basic ministry is pastoral in nature, and those who care for the life of the person present for ministry will have both the best insight and spiritual gifts to minister. Furthermore, to isolate one stage is to risk a serious distortion or imbalance in gospel living.

When repentance and conversion are the sole approach, the person is called to make good decisions about his life but he may reduce all to a willpower approach. This could result in a Pelagian approach to living—the attitude that everything depends on man's actions, and not on the power of the Holy Spirit. Such a willpower approach could fail to invoke the authority given by Jesus and could therefore be impotent against infestations of evil.

When deliverance is the only action taken in the ministry, the strong authority invoked against the kingdom of evil could prove ineffectual if there has not been the repentance and conversion needed to withdraw the right by which the evil spirits are present. Furthermore, to stop with deliverance is to leave voids in the person's life. The person still needs healing and spiritual strengthening.

When healing is the sole approach, there is often a strong petition and openness to receive graces and gifts. However, there is a danger of a passive Christianity in which repentance, decision to commit, grow, and to use God-given authority are not employed. This tendency can be very subtle if the person is having good experiences in healing prayer. While the reliving of past experiences, the ventilation of repressed emotions, and the accompanying prayerful support can bring temporary comfort and freedom, they are not sufficient to effect permanent change in attitude and action. It is sadly true that even while using Christian terminology, it is possible for healing prayer experiences to be no different than secular sensitivity sessions.

In fact, some healing sessions can be overwhelmingly an experience of Freudian psychotherapy and only incidentally an experience of relying on the power of God.

We believe that the pastoral care approach will prevent overlooking any important elements and will lead to the best balance in ministry. It is interesting that in the New Testament the Greek word for deliverance, "sotsot," also means salvation, healing, and related actions of saving grace. Our ministry should always have the dimension of "sotsot."

Whenever the deliverance ministry operates apart from a system of pastoral care, those responsible for the ministry must exert extraordinary effort to establish a special support system to provide continuing care. Without this support, there is a high probability that the person will fall back into the former state of bondage.

The deliverance ministry session itself should bring together all the elements of the system of pastoral care which support the individual. The purpose of much of the rest of this section is to describe a procedure for the deliverance session—and for the overall context of pastoral care—which has worked best for us. We do not maintain that the deliverance session must follow the pattern described here exactly. However, we do believe that the elements of the session, reflecting the system of pastoral care, should be present if the deliverance ministry is to be and remain effective.

Who Should Be Present?

The person in charge of the session should be the one who has some overall pastoral authority over the person present for ministry. If there is a person with more immediate pastoral authority such as parents for children, husband for his wife, or a local pastoral head or assistant pastor, this person should also be present. Normally the person in charge of the session will endeavor to have someone else present to assist him. This person should have recognized pastoral authority and experience in deliverance ministry. Finally, if the person present for ministry is a woman, then another woman who would be most helpful both in the session and the follow-up, taking both into consideration, should be present.

Format

While no two sessions are alike, an effective deliverance ministry should incorporate seven elements or stages. These stages do not have to be followed rigidly, one after another. But all stages should be present because all seven are important parts of the pastoral care for the person present for ministry. The goal of the session is the person's spiritual freedom and growth. The goal is not to do a specific form of prayer or to employ any set schema of word or actions, nor is it to mechanically implement a standard remedy for a problem diagnosed before the session.

An analogy will be helpful. We can compare this ministry to a doctor's care for a person who has been in an auto accident. The doctor would check many possible injuries. Depending on the person's condition, the doctor would have many treatments to choose from, ranging from surgery to rest. One of the doctor's main responsibilities is to see that all possibilities have been covered and that the correct treatment has been prescribed.

Effective deliverance follows a similar pattern. The model format for overall pastoral care serves as a check list to insure that the deliverance ministry will include the necessary elements. These seven stages are: (1) Preparation, (2) Introduction, (3) Listening, (4) Repentance, (5) Deliverance, (6) Healing-Blessing, and (7) Pastoral Guidance.

Preparation

The first step in the format is preparation. The person to receive ministry should have made all the decisions possible to put his or her life in order. The person should have repented from all serious sin and received forgiveness. He should have committed his life to Jesus as Lord and Savior and, insofar as possible, prayed to be baptized in the Holy Spirit and to have the spiritual gifts released in his life. He should have attempted to put his family, church, and business life in order according to scriptural principles. He should have attempted to come under pastoral authority and to implement the guidance of that authority in his life.

Of course, the work of evil spirits in the person's life—the very basis for needing deliverance ministry—may impede one or more of these standards from being achieved. When this happens, it is clear where the blockage is taking place. However, it is essential to examine other possible explanations for deficiencies in the person's life. Has the person heard the Good News, received proper teaching, been called to repent and to commit his or her life fully to the Lord? If these things have not happened, it is much more difficult to discern the presence of evil spirits. During this time of preparation, it might be appropriate to pray for a specific inner healing. The relationship between inner healing and deliverance is developed in Chapter Seven.

This time of preparation may take considerable time, but eventually the person and the one caring for him may conclude that there is need for deliverance. It will be clear to them that further progress either requires or will be greatly aided by deliverance ministry. The person should be told that this ministry is a normal step in growing in the Christian life. Original sin makes all people subject to the dominion of Satan, the prince of the world. Evil spirits can affect our lives even after we have become Christians because we are involved in a struggle between two kingdoms.

The person preparing for deliverance ministry and the one giving pastoral care should prepare with prayer and perhaps fasting. Through such prayer, God will frequently give spiritual insight accompanied by the fruits of the Holy Spirit. Even when no further insight is needed, such preparation will strengthen everyone spiritually for the ministry session. All who will be involved in the ministry should make some appropriate spiritual preparation.

The time and place for deliverance ministry should be carefully chosen. It is usually a mistake to minister at a time and place determined by the manifestation of the problem. The time and place should be our choosing, not that of evil spirits. The place chosen should be a place blessed and set aside for ministry. It should be a private place, free from interruptions. The time should be one in which all involved can ultilize full spiritual resources without pressure or fatigue or time limits. Nevertheless, the session should be planned to end within a reasonable period of time, usually two hours.

Finally, whenever possible, a group of intercessors should support the ministry. This group needs only to know that the ministry is scheduled for a particular time. The names of the people to be ministered to and the details of the ministry should usually be kept confidential by those directly involved.

Those leading the ministry should themselves also intercede before and during the ministry. This need is clearly under-scored by Jesus' teaching in Mark's Gospel: When the disciples tried to cast out the evil spirit from the mute boy and failed, they asked Jesus, "Why is it that we could not expel it?" He replied, "This kind you can drive out only by prayer" (Mk 9:28-29).

Introduction

The second step is the introduction. The person in charge of the session should make clear the role of each person present. He should explain that he will be responsible for all decisions and the exercise of all authority. He will explain how others present may assist him in this. He should say that the individ-ual who has the most immediate pastoral care for the person present for ministry is responsible for insuring that all relevant information is presented. This individual is also responsible for recording what takes place during the session so that the per-son can be cared for in the future. The leader will urge the person present for ministry to be open with his or her life, and to take maximum initiative. The person to be prayed with should be open about whatever is going on inside in order for those present to be effective in ministry. At the same time, he should be active in renouncing evil spirits and commanding them to depart. A forceful person will need less assistance from others in exercising authority. If the person undergoing ministry is not free to decide and command clearly and forcefully, others can ordinarily supply what is lacking. In some cases the leader will determine that the ministry should be halted.

The session should begin with prayer by all present. Special prayers for protection should be said for each person. We usually sprinkle holy water around the room and over those present. While some spiritual preparations are necessary, they should not create a rigid or artificial atmosphere. It is important that all present be able to communicate normally.

Listening and Discerning

The listening and discerning stage is crucial to the success of the session. Ordinarily, the ministers receive discernment about the presence of specific evil spirits because they listen both to what the person tells them and to what the Holy Spirit reveals to them. The person undergoing ministry should explain how he or she experiences blocks and recurrent difficulties. The person in immediate pastoral care should guide the explanations so that the most important facts are presented. The person in overall pastoral authority for the session should ask questions and receive suggestions about further questions from the others present.

The people present ordinarily possess some special gifts of revelation by which they can identify problems with precision. This can be of great benefit, but the ministry should basically operate under the overall authority of the person pastoring the session. His decisions are to be final.

Many factors come into play in arriving at the conclusion that specific evil spirits are involved in the person's life. Some of this information is revealed directly by the Holy Spirit. Other signs will be noticed by those present: patterns of irrational behavior, words which convey unreasonably strong power or emotion, the presence of a personality foreign to the person speaking, or sudden changes in personality when a particular area is discussed.

It is very important to identify the area under the control or influence of an evil spirit. Thus, by a spirit of anger we mean a spirit which influences the way in which a particular person becomes angry or expresses anger. A spirit of lust would influence the way in which a person becomes sexually aroused or pursues his or her desires. A spirit of fear would pertain to responses of becoming afraid and the ways in which such fear is expressed. We are not necessarily referring in this book to what would be proper names of evil spirits. What we are interested in doing is identifying them in a manner sufficient to expel them.

Further, these areas of operation usually involve more than one activity; what is most commonly experienced is an overlapping of a number of activities. Thus a spirit of bitterness may also involve resentment, hatred, retaliation, or unforgiveness. A spirit of rebellion may involve the presence of stubbornness and disobedience. A spirit of depression may involve discouragement, despair, hopelessness, suicide, and despondency. A spirit of insecurity may involve inferiority, loneliness, inadequacy, and self-pity. A spirit of guilt may involve self-condemnation, shame and unworthiness. It is important to know that there are a number of spirits that can cluster in this manner. One name in the cluster is frequently the key to freeing up the person. One of the names, usually the first listed above, will be sensed by the ministers as the right area to be dealt with. Then the other spirits in the cluster may or may not have to be dealt with individually.

This listening and discernment stage is concluded with the leader summarizing the discernment. He should help those present reach agreements about what is involved and how it should be handled. He should initiate an agreed course of action and propose an analysis of the problem and the spirit or spirits to be handled. This is not to exclude further developments that may take place in the ministry, nor need it specify details of everything that will transpire. However, he should present a general outline and those persons present at the session should agree to it. Their agreement will enable everyone to be praying and acting in a mutually supportive way. It will also prepare the person receiving ministry to take initiative at the right time without hesitation or confusion as to what is happening.

Repentance

Repentance is often overlooked by those who assume that the person in bondage has repented of all sins. Frequently, the listening stage has revealed areas of unrepented and unforgiven sin. The person could be actively nursing resentment or hatred, or he or she may not want to discontinue immoral sexual relationships or sinful addictions. Frequently, the person may not have forgiven someone because he thought he had to *feel* forgiveness before he could forgive. The person needs to know that repentance means a commitment to act righteously and to change sinful behavior. An emotion of sorrow is not the primary requirement in repentance.

Catholics and other Christians believing in the Sacrament of Penance should utilize the sacrament, at least for serious sin. If a priest is present, confession can take place as part of the ministry. If no priest will be present, confession should precede the ministry session. Even where there has been an earlier confession, this repentance stage should not be omitted.

Whether confession takes place before the ministry or at an interval during the ministry, the seal of confession obviously must apply for the priest involved. Furthermore, strict confidentiality must be maintained on all matters by those involved in the deliverance ministry session, and finally, any notes or material written during the session should come under the same bonds of confidentiality.

On occasion a person will state that he or she cannot forgive someone or cannot repent for a certain sin. Repentance here is nevertheless necessary. A person may avoid repentance because a lying spirit has influenced them to this conclusion, because they do not understand repentance, or because they do not realize that they must forgive others who have not repented of their own sins. The leader of the session may decide that such a person should be prayed with for a contrite heart and a spirit of repentance.

Whatever the situation, our experience has been that the repentance stage can always be handled successfully with sufficient perseverence.

Frequently the stage of repentance concludes with the person renewing his or her commitment to Jesus as Savior and Lord.

Deliverance

The fifth stage is the ministry of deliverance from evil spirits. If he has not done so earlier, the leader should pray for the spiritual protection of all present. He should command all evil spirits in the name of Jesus to obey him.

The leader then directs the person to deal with a particular area. He instructs the person to renounce the evil spirit, to choose the spirit of holiness, and to command the evil spirit to leave. Thus he or she might say, "I renounce all spirits of resentment in my life; I decide to live according to God's commandment of forgiveness and love; and in the name of Jesus, I command you, spirit of resentment, to get out of my life and stay out." When the person so commands, the leader and others present join in the command. At times the group or family of spirits will have to be dealt with before those present have a sense that the spirit has been cast out. Thus after casting out resentment, those present may then attack spirits of hatred, envy, or retaliation if such a family or cluster of spirits is discerned to be present.

Though it is unlikely, it is possible that at this point the leader may discern that the person is possessed (see Chapter Six). In such a situation he should proceed no further but bind all evil and end the ministry session. In the case of possession, it is essential to secure the full authorization of Church authorities to proceed. For Roman Catholics this means that the local bishop must confirm the nature of the case and appoint a priest to serve as exorcist. For Christians who have committed their lives to the Lord and undergone the preparation stage described above, it would be surprising to find that they are possessed.

There should be a natural flow to the deliverance ministry. There should be no rush to push on, nor should those present anxiously attempt to cast out every possible spirit. The session should be marked by confidence in the Lord, trusting that he will reveal whatever should be handled.

This stage ends when there is a spiritual sense that the spirits have been cast out. The person being prayed with normally states that he is at peace with no disturbance within him. Frequently, he will mention a prayerful spirit or a desire to praise God.

Healing and Blessing

The sixth stage is prayer for healing and blessing. In this stage we ask God to bring healing wherever there is a lack of wholeness in the person and to bless the person with the spiritual gifts and strengthening graces he or she needs.

Our experience is that these prayers are always needed. When there has been a deliverance, there has been a casting out and there is in some way a void remaining. This void should be filled in. Thus a person who has been delivered from spirits in the areas of resentment, bitterness, hatred, and unforgiveness should be prayed with for a healing of relationships. The person should ask for God's love to flow into that area and be the foundation of a new love for those he formerly resented or hated. The prayer may be simply stated just in those words. For imaginative and intuitive people, particularly women, the minister can lead the person to imagine the healing. The person can picture the Lord, then the Lord loving him, then the Lord loving the person resented, and finally, the Lord loving them both and bringing them together. This picture process illustrates the truth of what God's grace should accomplish in our lives. Our love for others is based on God first loving us; we then receive God's love for those we find impossible to love on our own. God's love is a gift to us. In turn, his love is the basis for our loving others.

If a particular circumstance or event has caused the person to open himself to the influence of evil spirits, the ministers should pray for the inner healing of the memory of this event. For instance, we have encountered a number of cases of women who were raped being later afflicted by spirits of fear and hatred of men. Once these spirits have been cast out, it is most helpful to pray with the woman for the healing of the memory of the rape. We have found that the woman can experience the presence of a loving God assuring her that he will take care of her and bring her healing, new life, and fullness of life forever. This presence and gift of love from God, applied to the memory of the horrifying events of the rape, can overcome the violent experience. Most women in these circumstances so experience God present in the memory that whenever they remember the rape, it no longer carries with it the power to stir up fear and hatred.

We have used this process effectively to heal childhood memories of being abandoned by parents, childhood memories of being locked in a cellar or closet, memories of violent crime, memories of sexually perverted acts, memories of deeply humiliating sins, and memories of traumatic betrayals by parents, friends, family, teachers, or business associates. In all cases, the memory has power to disturb the person because it is completely associated with destructive or negative experiences. Once the memory has been opened to an experience of God's love for the person, this totally negative nature of the memory is changed.

This opening of the memory to an experience of God's love is not artificial but, rather, places the memory in the framework of reality. It is a fact that the events of rape, abandonment, abuse, and betrayal take place in a world situation in which God is present and is offering his love. This type of prayer releases the power of the Holy Spirit into areas which had been shielded from God's love and the presence of his Spirit. The persons so prayed with will frequently remark that they experience being washed clean and renewed.

This prayer of release of the Holy Spirit is one among other prayers of blessing appropriate for this stage of the deliverance session. Prayers of blessing are prayers that God will give spiritual gifts and help for particular areas of a person's life. It is appropriate to pray for specific gifts of the Holy Spirit found in scripture: wisdom, fortitude, fear of the Lord, perseverence, peace, joy, faithfulness, love, patience, self-control.

The prayers for God's help are usually more specific: "Lord we ask you to bless John that he may be protected from temptations of envy at work, and from temptations to lust when he sees the covers of magazines." Prayers may be said for protection during a difficult journey or through the night. Prayers may be for a person to control his anger or for freedom from a desire to conquer others.

The prayers for healing and blessing may also include prayers for physical healing. Many physical problems can be healed once the person has been delivered from evil spirits and has experienced inner healing. We have seen healings at this time from asthma, chronic back pain, eye twitching, ulcers, stomach disturbance and arthritis. Finally, all present should be prayed with for protection from harassment by evil spirits. The spirits should be forbidden to bother anyone present.

Pastoral Guidance

The final and seventh stage is pastoral guidance. It is exceedingly important that there be: (1) a plan for follow-up care; (2) a specific person or persons responsible for the plan; and (3) a clear explanation of the plan and its importance.

The plan should involve practical steps to build up the life of the person in those areas which have been the object of ministry and to protect the person from falling back into sins or situations whereby he could come under the influence of evil spirits. The specifics of the plan will vary from person to person. For one person it may be a specific daily schedule; for another, restrictions on recreation areas or certain associations with friends; for others, daily phone calls or visits with the one who has pastoral care for the person. Frequently the plan will include a specific form of prayer or a specified area of scripture study. Some people may need to study areas of Christian formation or to read a particular book. In nearly all cases there is a specific type of temptation that needs to be dealt with in an agreed upon manner. It is common to review the person's spiritual commitments and to adjust them according to the needs that have become apparent through the ministry.

Once a person has been delivered from evil spirits, he is ready to make decisions to change his patterns of thinking and acting. Deliverance destroys the root of Satan's hold in a particular area, but it does not automatically change a person's patterns of living. It is necessary for the person to decide on the new patterns and exercise personal authority daily to adhere to them.

For example, a person may habitually avoid persons and places out of a spirit of fear. Casting out the spirit of fear will not change the habit of avoiding others, unless the individual decides to change the habit. People freed of addiction to drink will still feel like drinking as an answer to personal problems. People freed of a spirit of insecurity will still tend to do all the things they ever did to please people and receive affirmation. It is necessary to recognize the new freedom, decide not to respond to temptations to act in old ways, and live out this decision through the exercise of daily personal authority. Pastoral care involves helping people change their feelings and their patterns of life to reflect their new freedom.

At the beginning of this chapter, three case histories were summarized. In all three, the leader of the session used a card to record the principal points of the ministry and the main points of agreement about future pastoral care. This card has been very useful in enabling the person and the one giving pastoral care to review their progress together after the ministry session. The card contains the following categories:

Root Problem (source of problem; specific events or situations) and response to problem (person's initial movements; fear, anger, lust, etc.).

Bondage (area of person's life bound by evil in some way) and manifestations (behavior reflecting lack of freedom).

Ministry Repentance: (sinful behavior repented) Deliverance: (spirits delivered) Healing and blessings: (specific prayers for healing and blessing).

Pastoral direction (agreed commitments for ongoing growth).

Persons can use the card to determine whether there is continual growth or whether there are relapses into old problems as evidenced by responses and manifestations. The form of the card should be altered whenever it will improve the clarity of the recording of information.

Getting Started

Groups which want to establish a deliverance ministry should give careful thought about how to proceed. Since a system of overall pastoral care is necessary if the ministry is to be effective, this discussion of getting started is directed to groups, not individuals.

One general principle can be stated: Groups should not attempt deliverance unless they are solidly committed, have recognized leaders who can give direction to the group members, and can provide sufficient pastoral care to handle follow-up with people who have been prayed with.

The following guidelines are intended to help groups determine whether they are able to make use of deliverance and, if so, how to begin.

1. *Deliverance should take place in the context of overall pastoral care.* Groups should see deliverance as a pastoral tool enabling the leaders to care for the group and lead people to a deeper relationship with the Lord.

During deliverance, it is important for those doing the praying to have personal and pastoral knowledge of the person they are praying with. Because deliverance touches personal areas, it is important that the person being prayed with trust those praying with him. The gifts of revelation and discernment which operate in the prayer session are not meant to substitute for personal and pastoral knowledge, but to work with them to bring to the fore those areas in need of prayer. Deliverance sessions can also be a time for advice and counsel on how to continue to work on a particular area of sin or weakness.

Because of the pastoral nature of deliverance, the leaders of the group should be the ones who conduct prayer for deliverance. The pastoral skill, knowledge, and confidentiality involved usually require that this area not be given over to other members of the group.

There is a clear implication in all this: If a group does not have mature leadership, or if there are only loosely structured elements of commitment and responsibility, the group should not begin deliverance, since it does not have the necessary foundations for such a ministry.

2. *The leaders should come to a common mind about deliverance.* They should study the subject together and get their questions answered to a satisfactory degree. They should resolve any differences they may have. If the leadership is divided on whether to begin deliverance, they should wait until agreement is reached. Most important of all, the leaders should determine, through prayer and consultation, whether God wants the group to make use of deliverance in its pastoral care.

The leaders should be prayed with for deliverance themselves before they attempt to pray with others in the group. As well as being personally beneficial for the leaders, it will give them some good personal experience to work from.

3. *When beginning, those responsible should get experienced help.* Leaders ought not to think they have all the tools necessary to begin praying with people after reading one or two books about deliverance. Nothing can replace supervised training. The leaders should look for help from mature, experienced people in another group or community.

Where possible, the leaders of the group should travel to another group that has a solid deliverance ministry and learn as much as they can from them. While spending time with the other group, the leaders will be able to see the fruits of deliverance in that group and get their questions answered. This is where the leaders themselves should be prayed with. When they return to their own group, they should take time to evaluate their own experience.

A word of caution: Seek help from a group known to be solid, mature, experienced in deliverance. Very few groups have such qualifications. Much confusion and turmoil can result from learning wrong things from immature or misdirected groups.

4. *Start slowly.* Those beginning in deliverance should give themselves time to gain experience and confidence. If difficulties are encountered of such magnitude that the leaders find themselves over their heads, they should admit the problem and stop.

Prayer for deliverance should be directed mainly toward the more mature and stable individuals. It is a mistaken notion that deliverance should be aimed primarily at people with significant emotional and spiritual problems. It is true that, in the proper context, such people can derive great benefit from deliverance. But groups normally should not try to handle such cases; they should work with Christians whose lives are in basic order but who are experiencing resistance in some areas of life.

Similarly, deliverance is for people in the group, not for friends, relatives, or needy people in town. Those in deliverance should pray only with people for whom they have some direct and immediate pastoral responsibility.

Pray with people one at a time. Avoid any mass deliverance sessions. As far as pastoral care is concerned, mass deliverance sessions are not very helpful.

5. *Never force anyone to be prayed with.* At times, it may seem that deliverance is just what a particular person needs. That may be right. But if the person himself doesn't agree, he should not be pushed into it.

6. *The leaders should make sure that deliverance is handled in an orderly and peaceful way.* They should decide who to pray with, and not let circumstances dictate. A number of people think that deliverance is going to be the answer to their problems. They will want to be prayed with as soon as possible. Leaders should not yield to such pressure.

Leaders should exercise strong control over any outsiders who come to the group claiming to have a ministry of deliverance. Itinerant ministries are difficult to assess accurately and can cause harm in such personal areas as deliverance. No outside person should be allowed to pray with people in the group unless the leaders are confident in the person and his gift, and are willing to take the time to follow up with the people he prays with.

EIGHT

Discernment

Discernment is perhaps the most crucial element in deliverance. It is fundamentally a spiritual gift and as such cannot be learned or taught. The operation of the Holy Spirit through discernment keeps the deliverance session on track and provides the inspiration and insight necessary to know how to proceed. Discernment is the main guiding force in: (1) knowing what is actually the work of an evil spirit; (2) deciding what area to deal with next; (3) knowing whether the evil spirit is truly gone; (4) revealing the presence or activity of evil spirits not already known at the time the deliverance began; (5) determining at what pace the session should proceed and how long it should last; and (6) what other forms of ministry the person may need (inner healing, counsel, repentance, strengthening, and comfort).

While discernment is primarily a spiritual gift, it is also true that it is meant to work in tandem with the experience and knowledge of those ministering deliverance. The direction and counsel given during a deliverance session will be a blend of the natural and the supernatural elements. The store of experience, wisdom, and knowledge that the ministers bring to the deliverance session provides a crucial element in the discernment process which makes judgments more reliable. For example, having some experience in how certain emotional problems manifest themselves provides a protection against a hasty judgment about the presence of evil spirits based simply on external behavior. Again, knowing that eating habits can affect a person's ability to function (inability to concentrate, hyperactivity, sleeplessness), his physical condition (allergies, eczema), and his emotions (anxiety, irritability), enables the ministers to form proper judgments and to help the person in the right way (perhaps by referring him to a doctor or a nutritionist).

Because experience, wisdom, and knowledge play such an important role in deliverance, we again stress the importance of learning about deliverance from experienced people who can help those just beginning to avoid the mistakes and pitfalls which are the result of inexperience.

While discernment is a spiritual gift, some traits of demonic activity can be noticed and experience can aid the discernment process.

Characteristic Activity

People who have experience in the deliverance ministry agree that some evil spirits have identifiable patterns of activity which nearly always reveal their presence immediately. Such patterns become clear as the same spirits are encountered over a period of time during different deliverance sessions. The knowledge of these patterns and characteristics is a valuable aid in discernment. For example, certain habitual sins in bondage to evil spirits will leave the person in a state of abject and oppressive guilt after the sinful act. The evil spirits seem to delight in incessantly inciting a person to sin and then mercilessly condemning the person when he falls to the temptation. When we encounter someone under such oppressive guilt, it is almost certain that an evil spirit is behind the sinful habit.

Another characteristic of evil spirit activity is that certain spirits seem to cluster together. When we find a particular spirit, we can know with a high degree of certainty that some other particular spirits are present also. For example, when the demon of hate is found, anger, bitterness, and resentment are usually also present. (See the discussion of clusters of spirits in Chapter Seven, p. 86.)

We should be cautious about reaching conclusions from these two traits of demonic activity. Characteristic activity and clusters of spirits are not invariable principles of demonic behavior. Evil spirits can disguise their activity well, and they sometimes do not travel in clusters. Discernment remains the major source of guidance through deliverance.

Why Are Spirits Present?

Our experience has been that satanic activity in a person's life is often the result of an interaction between evil spirits, sin, emotional and psychological barriers and scars, developmental circumstances, personal strengths and weaknesses, and a person's will.

The dark areas of sin in a person's life are fertile ground for the activity of evil spirits. Both sin and its by-products, such as guilt and repression, can easily be brought under demonic bondage.

Basic emotional needs which are either unfulfilled or perceived by the person as unfulfilled can leave a person vulnerable to demonic influence. The subsequent effects of these unmet needs are also ready targets for evil spirits. Someone, for example, may feel unloved. This can lead to such problems as isolation and self-rejection which in turn are breeding grounds for evil spirits.

Certain traumatic events in a person's life can be a doorway for satanic entrance. We recall a deliverance session with a young woman in her mid-twenties for deliverance. Sheila asked, in a somewhat embarrassed manner, if we could pray for her fear of the dark. She had been afraid of the dark since she was a child, and even now, as a married woman with children, she had to have night lights in her bedroom at night. I asked if she could remember a specific time when she began to be afraid of the dark. She could remember it clearly. She used to sleep in the dark, but one night, when she was a young child, she woke up thoroughly disoriented. She couldn't find her way out of her dark bedroom to get to her parents, and became utterly terrified. From that time on, Sheila was afraid of the dark. After we prayed with Sheila for deliverance, she was no longer afraid of the dark.

Events such as these are a normal part of childhood and most people grow out of them. Sheila did not. Her fear is an example of a traumatic event which evil spirits can use to turn normal problems into insurmountable obstacles. We can identify such cases through discernment, supported by certain symptoms.

A number of times during deliverance, we have encountered an evil spirit which is present not because of any event or activity which the person participated in, but because of something or someone in the family's past. It's almost as though people sometimes inherit a vulnerability to certain evil spirits. The most effective way to deal with these spirits is to deny and void any claim the spirit has on the person because of his or her family. Then we cast out the spirit.

While praying with one young woman, we came upon a strong spirit of witchcraft which puzzled us. The woman said that she herself had had no serious involvement with the occult; only a brief childhood contact with a ouija board. However, she said her mother had been very much involved in the occult as long as she could remember. We were able to free the young woman from the evil spirit primarily by discrediting any claim the spirit had on the daughter because of the mother. We then cast it out.

Finally, many times evil spirits just are there. There does not seem to be any reason why a particular spirit should have this person in bondage, and yet it does. We simply cast it out. Much time can be wasted trying to understand how a particular spirit works in a person. If there is no immediate obvious reason and the Lord doesn't give us any revelation or discernment on the matter, we cast the spirit out and move on.

Evil Spirits as Part of the Self

When evil spirits have been in a person for many years, the person is usually unaware of their presence. As a result, his personal formation and basic self-image tend to accommodate the evil spirit's presence and activity. Thus, what someone may believe is his or her basic personality may in fact be a mixture of the actual person and evil spirits. Helping a person disentangle this mixture during a deliverance session is often a complicated matter.

Perhaps the most common example of this phenomenon is the personality of the individual who sees himself as basically unlovable. Many people we have prayed with have some reason for seeing themselves as unlovable; they have had poor childhoods and their parents and friends really did concretely reject them. But self-rejection also regularly occurs in people who had basically very warm, supportive, and accepting childhoods. Nothing in their past lives explains their problems with basic self-rejection.

In the latter cases, an evil spirit is often at the core of the problem. These spirits manage to get into the person's life in many ways, but the point is that the person experiences the difficulty as one of self, not the working of an evil spirit. "I am unlovable," he claims. In the person's own mind, the spirit and the self become one.

The individual is often unable to detect such evil spirits because they operate at the level of half-truth and twist it to their own ends. For example, they cause an insecure person to be overly sensitive to the smallest offenses committed against him. They will twist a normal, innocent oversight in personal relationships into a seeming act of rejection, thus further solidifying the basic problem.

It is important to emphasize again that evil spirit activity of this sort mimics the psychological workings of a problem with insecurity. To some extent this is true; part of what is going on is psychological. But what is behind such insecurity, giving it force and a compelling nature, is an evil spirit which has made itself seem what it is not—the individual's own personality.

Camouflage

Evil spirits can make a pleasant home for themselves in a person's life. When a grain of sand is introduced into the sensitive body of an oyster, the oyster will surround it with layers of pearl. In the same way, we can wrap an evil spirit in something nice, thus hiding the foreign element and instead producing what appears to be a treasure.

I (Cirner) was praying with a man in his mid-thirties for deliverance a couple of years ago. His name is Bret. During the session, he brought up the fact that he felt very misunderstood. Bret thought that he had often not been given the kind of opportunities to make use of his talents that he thought he deserved. Bret said that people at work and in the community didn't know how to handle him because he was creative and didn't fit into molds.

Bret had been having a good amount of difficulty at work. He just couldn't seem to get along with his boss, and his attempts at what he considered "creative initiative" usually met with resistance. He had a similar problem in the community. He considered his manner of speaking and his ways of doing things to be expressions of his creative nature. For example, when someone in authority would ask him to do something for him a certain way, Bret would do it the way *he* wanted to—not the way he was asked to do it.

Bret was genuinely creative—not nearly to the extent he thought—but he did have talents. However, it was clear to me that Bret's analysis of the problem was wrong; something else was going on underneath all of this.

As we continued to pray and talk, the Lord showed me that what was really going on was that Bret was basically undisciplined and rebellious. His creativity, while partly genuine, was mainly a camouflage through which his basic rebellion was free to operate. As we talked about it, Bret was able to confirm my thinking. He said that the roots of the rebellion went back into his childhood. He had felt cheated because his father died soon after Bret was born, and his mother had had to work hard to support the family. The resulting sense of loneliness and confusion led Bret to decide never to put himself in the position of being hurt again. Because of the family situation, neither Bret's mother nor anyone else could give Bret the formation he needed. He wandered through his early years with few restraints on him, an easy prey for evil spirits. By the time he finished high school, Bret was convinced that the rest of the world didn't know how to adapt to his creativity. It never occurred to him that the root problem was with him, not with the rest of the world.

Such camouflage is not always in the form of an apparent virtue such as creativity. Sometimes evil spirits may use lesser difficulties to hide the real problem. For example, anxiety, while not pleasant, is a socially acceptable problem and can often mask the more serious problem of guilt. A short temper, often a quite acceptable trait, can mask bitterness and resentment.

Sometimes evil spirits become thoroughly entrenched within a person, and they do not immediately leave when commanded to go. There are three major reasons for this:

1. *Unrepented sin.* Where the person has made a conscious or even unconscious alliance with sin, evil spirits seem to have a right of access and possession. They work under cover of spiritual darkness. When a person's life is in darkness, sin needs to be brought to the light through renunciation and acceptance of God's forgiveness. Repentance brings darkness into the light, and removes any foothold for the evil spirit.

2. *Unwillingness to change behavior.* Sometimes the key to living righteously is tied to a decision to change behavior patterns. People can experience a strong resistance to this because it entails a change in the way they view themselves.

For example, a man may view himself as a strong, independent thinker, a trait which leads him consistently into wrong judgments and behavior, and which he acknowledges as a problem. However, he may be so invested in this image of himself as the strong, independent type, that he is closed to suggestions and guidance from others.

Another reason for this unwillingness may be a strong attachment to a particular form of sin. We once prayed with a young man who had a serious problem with sexual immorality. During the prayer session, he mentioned that he had to walk past an adult bookstore on his way to work every day. He found that he couldn't resist looking at the window displays;

this only reinforced his immoral desires. We said, "Don't walk past the bookstore. Walk a different way." The young man thought of many reasons why he could not change his route to work. The evil spirit of sexual immorality would not leave until the man finally decided to not walk past that bookstore. It is clear that flirting with the near occasion of sin is enough to give evil spirits a hold.

3. *Part of a complex cluster of things.* Sometimes an evil spirit is able to take root in a person's life as firmly as a tree secures itself to the earth in a tangle of roots. At times like these it is almost impossible to use a simple word of command to expel him. Rather, those ministering deliverance need to dig around and loosen up the areas around the evil spirit. Through repentance, prayer for inner healing (the removal of emotional scars and bondages), confessions of faith, and counsel, the roots which keep the evil spirit anchored in the person's life are severed, the tap root is unearthed and cut, and the once immovable evil spirit is finally cast out.

We have found this type of situation in cases where there seemed to be a ruling spirit present. The ruling spirit is a dominant spirit who usually has some influence over the other evil spirits present. His own particular nature is usually somehow obvious in the behavior of the person, such as pride, fear, anger, lust, and the occult. However, the ruling spirit has surrounded himself with lesser spirits in an intricate system of deception and confusion. In these cases, deliverance depends upon a high degree of discernment and patient determination.

Protection Against Evil Spirits

In dealing with evil spirits, we have found that an effective defense against their return can be maintained. This defense consists of: (1) righteous living, that is, avoiding sin; (2) changing potentially harmful behavior patterns; (3) knowing and accepting the truth of our life in God; (4) acknowledging our vulnerability to evil spirits; (5) strengthening areas of emotional and spiritual weakness through a deepening relationship with the Lord by using prayer, scripture, the sacraments; and (6) becoming part of a Christian group which is able to be of support.

Our experience has been that evil spirits return only when the remedial steps are lacking or present only in a weak form. Our experience here lines up with Jesus' warning that it is not enough just to clean out the house. If we clear a person's life of evil spirits but nothing positive comes to take their place, that person remains an easy target for worse things than have already been experienced. Satan is prevented any further return only when God's life is present and effectively being lived. (See Luke 11:24-26.)

Convalescence After Deliverance

When someone has major surgery for the removal of a tumor, a period of convalescence is necessary afterward. The tumor has harmed the body. The body has been depleting its resources fighting the intrusion of the tumor. After surgery, the body is weak and in need of rest. It is more susceptible to disease and infection until it has regained strength. The incisions are painful. There may even be some residual pain from the area where the tumor has been removed. The body needs time to recover.

There seems to be a spiritual counterpart to this. After someone has been prayed with for deliverance, the person may experience a few days of disconcerting turmoil which can cause confusion about the effectiveness of the deliverance. These may include feelings of condemnation and rejection, fears that things will not change at all, and some slight depression. Alarmingly, some problems may seem to reassert themselves more intensely than ever. This usually lasts for only a brief period, but it is a very important time. The person needs to receive the help of others who can speak the truth to him, help him understand what is happening, and pray with him. In a matter of a day or two, the person has usually regained his equilibrium and is able to experience his new freedom fully. At this point he is able to begin building effective defenses against evil spirits.

Oppression and Obsession

It is necessary in discernment to make a distinction between obsession and oppression. In obsession, evil spirits or demons have infested a particular area of a person's life. They are *not*, however, in possession of the person. On the other hand, they are not outside the person hassling him. Obsession is usually cause for deliverance ministry as described in this book.

Oppression is the experience of evil spirits pressing in on the person from the outside, causing heaviness, weariness, or discouragement. The remedy for oppression is to command the spirit of oppression to be gone in the name of Jesus. Normally, one command is sufficient and the person suffering oppression experiences an immediate lifting followed by a new sense of peace and joy. Oppression can happen through a variety of situations but usually the person oppressed has not opened himself to any particular spirit but has only exposed himself to circumstances in which there was a heavy presence of evil. We have known people to be oppressed as a result of participating in a deliverance session, being in an area where occult activities were transpiring, being placed under a curse or coming in contact with items of witchcraft. There have been other times when the causes were not determined.

The important difference between oppression and obsession is that in oppression the force is outside the person and is broken through a simple command, whereas in obsession the force is in the person and needs normally to be identified and to be cast out.

Situational Evil Spirits

We have found that evil spirits are able to influence people and events by influencing an environment. When spirits operate in this way they set a tone, create a mood, or directly control a few people in order to influence many others.

Sometimes we see obvious work of Satan when he uses the greed and madness of a few men to unleash the evil spirits of war. Twice in this century, he has plunged mankind into global conflict, and the possibility of another world war remains with us. Evil spirits also can stir up smaller wars and civil wars. The human element in war must not be denied, but it is clear that Satan is implicated in such conflict.

There are many other examples of major national and worldwide moods, trends, activities, and ideas which we believe are fueled and empowered by the activity of evil spirits. Satan is involved in that exalted pride in technological accomplishment which only strengthens man's delusion that he is independent of the Lord. Evil spirits are also highly invested in situations much closer to our daily lives. Spirits of sexual immorality and lust infest many places of entertainment—bars, discos, theaters. Walk into an occult bookstore and the oppression of evil spirits can literally be felt. The hostility, mistrust, and disunity found in many families and in other relationships surely have satanic backing.

An important aspect of the situational influence of evil spirits is the way they act to block the direct action of God. Since, at root, satanic malevolence is directed at God, it is logical that those situations, events, plans, and people which are more immediately related to the Lord and his purpose would be under greater attack by Satan.

At times, evil spirits will try to thwart God's plan by gently and patiently nudging something until it becomes hopelessly off course. The secularization of much of Western Christianity was brought about in just such a way. The process is still going on today, and evil spirits are giving it all the help they can.

As was stated at the beginning of the chapter, patterns of evil spirit activity discussed here are not *invariable* principles of behavior. Spirits do know how to disguise their activity well. Thus, in all these areas, discernment obviously remains the most crucial factor. Because discernment is so important, we advise, as is evident in the pastoral model, that those serving in deliverance ministry work in teams of at least two so that a single person does not have to rely totally on their own discernment.

NINE

Special Issues in Deliverance

In this chapter we will discuss several special issues which often need to be understood in the deliverance ministry. The issues discussed are: (1) sacraments and sacramentals; (2) inner healing; (3) deliverance and psychology; (4) use of authority when lacking experience; and (5) physical manifestations.

Sacraments and Sacramentals

Sacraments and sacramentals have a definite role in helping us become free of evil spirits. This can be accomplished in several ways. Generally, they help us grow in the holiness which creates a spiritual climate for driving out evil spirits. Thus, any growth in leading a holy life through prayerful participation in the sacraments or the use of sacramentals such as the crucifix, blessed oil, and holy water for protection against evil will be helpful.

More specifically, however, the sacraments and sacramentals have a far more significant role than simply affecting a spiritual climate or increase in piety.

The sacraments are intended to place the person in direct contact with the person and action of Jesus Christ.

At Baptism, Jesus is acting as Savior in the life of the person being baptized. In Confirmation, he is strengthening the person through the gifts of the Holy Spirit. In Matrimony, he is sealing the marriage with grace. In Holy Orders, he is accepting the commitment of the priest and the bishop and empowering him to preach, teach, and pastor. In the sacrament of Penance, Jesus forgives and, through the power of the Holy Spirit, reconciles the sinner to God and to the Church. In the Eucharist, the sacrifice of Jesus is reenacted, and then Jesus feeds the Body with his body and blood. In the Anointing of the Sick, Jesus is healing the sick of physical and spiritual disease. God ordained the sacraments as a means of direct contact with the Lord and Savior. This direct contact with the Lord and his holiness is powerful enough to free us from evil spirits if we are disposed in the right way and seeking such freedom. Frequently, however, the sacraments do not accomplish this because we are unable to utilize their power effectively.[29]

Sacramentals have a special place in spiritual warfare. Sacramentals are objects such as water and oil, set aside by the Church to be means or instruments of grace. Water is such a sacramental when it is blessed for use in repentance, Baptism, or for blessing people, places, or things. The sacramental is not a magical device which can operate on its own. Rather, it is an extension of the prayer of the Body of Christ through the pastoral authority of the Church. When the authorized minister prays over the water, the Church says:

> God's creature, water, I cast out the demon from you in the name of God the Father almighty, in the name of Jesus Christ His Son and Lord and in the power of the Holy Spirit. May you be a purified water, empowered to drive afar all power of the enemy, in fact, to out and banish the enemy himself along with his fallen angels. We ask this through the power of our Lord Jesus Christ who is coming to judge both the living and the dead and the world by fire. (*Roman Ritual*, p.396)

Similarly, the Church prays over the oil to be used in prayer for healing in these words:

> Lord God almighty, before whom the hosts of angels stand in awe and whose heavenly service we acknowledge; may it

please you to regard favorably and to bless and hallow this creature, oil, which by your power has been pressed from the juice of olives.

You have ordained it for anointing the sick so that when they are made well they may give thanks to you, the living and true God. Grant we pray that those who will use this oil, which we are blessing in your name, may be delivered from all suffering, all infirmity and all wiles of the enemy. Let it be a means of averting any kind of adversity from man, made in your image and redeemed by the precious blood of your Son so that he may never again suffer the sting of the ancient serpent; through Christ, Our Lord. (Ibid, p.573)

These blessings of baptismal water and oil date back in the life of the Church to the period immediately following the Apostolic Age. While sacramentals have been abused at times, by attributing to them an almost magical power, they have been more frequently used properly, as extensions of the intercessory prayer of the Church. We should view sacraments and sacramentals as very powerful sources and instruments of grace. They are resources to be used in spiritual warfare. However, it is not sufficient to simply concentrate on sacraments and sacramentals, believing that the forces of evil will thereby be driven away. This may happen, but it is frequently necessary to directly confront evil spirits, to renounce any basis for their presence, and to command them to leave. This is done very effectively in conjunction with sacraments and sacramentals.[30]

Inner Healing

One of the issues frequently raised is the relationship between deliverance and inner healing. In order to put some boundaries on the discussion, we want to emphasize that for the purpose of this book we are concerned with inner healing only to the extent that it relates to the deliverance ministry. We deal with inner healing in only two aspects. The first is during the stage of preparation, when prayers for specific needs are acknowledged as part of the preparation for the deliverance ministry. The second aspect is during the sixth stage of the deliverance ministry when prayers for inner healing are often used effectively following the deliverance. We discussed these general approaches to inner healing prayer, along with examples, in Chapter Seven.

Even within the framework of this discussion there remain two questions about inner healing. First, can there be an inner healing ministry session structured similarly to the deliverance session but independent of it? Yes, at times this is appropriate, as one of us indicated in a very early book on this ministry (Scanlan, *Inner Healing*, Paulist Press, 1974). At the same time, it would be a serious mistake to consider inner healing apart from the total pastoral care system. Especially important are basic commitment to the Lord, repentance, deliverance, and pastoral direction. It is a mistake, sometimes a dangerous mistake, to treat inner healing in isolation. There is a tendency in the inner healing ministry to see most problems as exclusively based in past negative experiences wherein the resultant memories or emotional scars need to be healed.

With this perspective, the individual can then become a passive patient who submits his life to the inner healing expert. Such an approach mitigates the effectiveness of sound teaching in Christian formation, the exercise of self-direction in the victory of Jesus Christ, the utilization of the power flowing from the release of the Holy Spirit, the effectiveness of deliverance in expelling evil spirits and the importance of pastoral guidance in living in accordance with God's plan. So just as this book emphasizes deliverance within the context of total pastoral care, so inner healing must be within this total concept. (See the discussion of the Pastoral Care approach, Chapter Seven.)

A second question is whether inner healing can replace the deliverance ministry. The answer is no. Like any prayer, inner healing prayer can expel evil spirits. However, there is nothing in inner healing prayer that would make it particularly effective when the proper remedy for the expulsion of evil spirits is to command them to leave. For this reason, during a deliverance session we have placed the stage for inner healing prayer after the stage for expelling evil spirits. We find that effective inner healing prayer can be blocked by the presence of evil spirits and is ordinarily more fruitful after evil spirits are expelled.

Deliverance and Psychology

One area of concern is the reconciliation of our approach to deliverance with current psychological theories about the source of behavior which deliverance has determined to be caused by evil spirits. There is admittedly definite tension between the two. However, we have asked a psychologist, Dr. Edward Herbert, to comment on this question. Dr. Herbert, who has participated in some of our ministry sessions, is a licensed psychologist and holds a doctorate in the field. He has reviewed the substance of this book. We quote from his analysis below:

> I have served with Father Scanlan at sessions of healing and deliverance and can testify to the efficacy of his pastoral approach. My participation in these sessions has been in the role of a supportive Christian brother, but I bring to such ministry in addition the eyes and mind of an experienced psychologist. I am registered in the state of Ohio as a licensed psychologist, and I hold an earned doctorate in the discipline. Even with years of psychological counseling, I have witnessed behavior in human beings in these sessions which exceeds the range normally considered by psychology. In other words, what the ministers of deliverance are dealing with is a reality which can not be effectively treated by psychotherapy.

> Thus, *Deliverance From Evil Spirits* is a welcome treatise for Christians concerned about the basic tenet of this book, i.e., the reality of Satan and his power. Theology intended for the layman has not treated this issue well, and sound, basic psychology has avoided the concern altogether. The approach to deliverance presented in this book is one that is

sound and well designed, one which can lead to greater freedom and mental health. My professional evaluation is that this approach will not engender false guilt or other psychological disturbances. On the contrary, under the leadership of mature Christians, I would expect it to produce substantial positive results.

Use of Authority When Lacking Experience

We often hear questions relating to situations in which a person needs deliverance, and the one who has pastoral responsibility for the person lacks the necessary experience or confidence to lead the deliverance ministry.

This situation does arise frequently, and therefore the ideal relationships cannot be established. In these circumstances, it is possible for the one pastoring the person needing deliverance to see that the preparation stage is completed and then to see that the pastoral direction is implemented. The person with immediate pastoral responsibilities can then seek someone with the authority to lead the deliverance session and submit to him for the ministry session but take full responsibility thereafter. This procedure should be approached with caution, however, because of the difficulty in maintaining consistency in pastoral authority.

Physical Manifestations

A number of physical manifestations of the presence of evil spirits can take place during a deliverance session. However, while physical manifestations can happen, usually deliverance occurs with almost no observable physical manifestations. Furthermore, most manifestations can be contained to a minimum by the firm authority of the one in charge. When manifestations need to be dealt with, they should not be given much importance, since they can distract from the main things God desires to have happen.

The most common manifestations we have seen are: restlessness (squirming, a desire to leave the room), drowsiness (yawning, mental lethargy), nausea, and sometimes facial and bodily contortions.

Speaking solely from our Western cultural perspective and experience, we believe that the three main factors in physical manifestations are the person's own strength of character, the level of love and trust between the subject and those praying with him, and expectations about manifestations.

1. Strength of character. By this we mean the level of maturity and formation in the natural and spiritual realms. When evil spirits are being commanded to leave, the person will generally have some internal emotion, experience, or thought such as fear or a heaviness being lifted or the words, "You can't make me go." Such internal happenings are usually the parting shot of the evil spirit as it leaves. When the person is someone who is basically a mature, self-controlled Christian, he is able to experience such things internally without external expression. However, when the person being prayed with does not have that basic self-control and maturity, he will usually handle internal experiences during deliverance the same way he handles his normal inner experiences—by yielding to them. Hence, the physical manifestations involved in deliverance are often the result of the lack of proper self-discipline.

2. Love and trust. Our experience has been that the greater the degree of love and trust between the person being prayed with and those ministering to him, the less tendency there is on the part of the person to be concerned about himself. As a result, he does not so closely monitor his own internal reactions. He is able to take a more objective view of the deliverance session. He can rely more on the faith of those praying with him to effect deliverance and thus has less need to look to physical manifestations as a sign. This brings us back again to the importance of the pastoral care context of deliverance.

3. Expectations. Most physical manifestations occur because that is what people have been told to expect and encouraged to yield to. When such expectations are not encouraged, there is a dramatic decrease in physical manifestations. Some ministers of deliverance who rely heavily on physical manifestations as a sign of deliverance point to the exorcisms of Jesus, notably the ones in Mark 1:23-26 and 9:17-26, to validate their expectations. It is important to keep in mind, however, that the scripture writers here were reporting what *did* happen, not necessarily what is *supposed* to happen, when evil spirits leave. Scripture is not a manual of deliverance. To insist on the basis of scripture, that there should be some physical evidence of the departure of an evil spirit is a misuse of the scripture texts. It is important to draw the distinction between what can happen and what should happen.

One final point should be made about physical manifestations. Our comments above apply to deliverance as we present it in this book. There are times when a person has been more radically taken over by an evil spirit and, as a result, has almost no ability to control his impulses. In such cases, the person in authority for the session must be the one to primarily control the evil spirit through commands. Sometimes, however, even the one in authority can't completely control the spirit, and the deliverance session gets a little colorful.

In these cases, we advise that if the ministers are experienced and confident in what they are doing, they can usually complete the deliverance without much trouble. Where experience and confidence are lacking, they should terminate the session and get some help.

Afterword

In conclusion, we emphasize again that the purpose of this book is primarily to aid those in positions of responsibility to grow in the pastoral care of brothers and sisters. Deliverance is not a ministry to be undertaken outside a body of committed Christians, nor by those who do not have clearly recognized authority within the body. Such standards are essential to the protection of all. As scripture says, "Our battle is not against human forces but against the principalities and powers, the rulers of the world of darkness, the evil spirits in regions above" (Eph 6:12). God has given us victory over such forces through the death and resurrection of Jesus Christ and by the power of his life within through Baptism. Our responsibility is to use that God-given authority in right order and with wisdom.

Notes

1. Justin Martyr, *The First Apology*, The Fathers of the Church, volume 6, The Catholic University of America Press, 1948, p. 96.

2. Origen, *The Fundamental Doctrines*, in *The Faith of the Early Fathers*, Collegeville: The Liturgical Press, ed. Jurgens, W.A., p. 192.

3. Cyprian, *Mortality*, The Fathers of the Church, volume 36, p 202.

4. Irenaeus, *Against Heresies*, Library of Fathers, Oxford: James Parker, 1872, p. 506.

5. Tertullian, *Apology*, The Fathers of the Church, volume 10, p. 69.

6. John Calvin, *Institutes of the Christian Religion I*, The Library of Christian Classics, volume 20, The Westminster Press, 1967, p. 174.

7. Pope Paul VI, General Audience, Nov. 1973.

8. Dom Robert Petitpierre, O.S.B., ed., *Exorcism*, Talbot Press (S.P.C.K.), Saffron Walden, Essex, England, 1972, pp. 11-13.

9. Adolf Rosewyk, *Possessed by Satan*, New York: Doubleday & Company, 1975, pp. 25-27.

10. Cyprian, *Mortality*, p. 202.

11. Cyprian, *Exhortation to Martyrdom, To Fortunatus*, The Fathers of the Church, volume 36, p. 314.

12. Justin Martyr, *The Second Apology*, The Fathers of the Church, volume 6, p. 124.

13. Augustine, *The Christian Combat*, The Fathers of the Church, volume 4, p. 316.

14. Cyril of Jerusalem, *The Catechetical Lectures*, Library of Christian Classics, volume 4, The Westminster Press, 1955, p. 96.

15. Justin Martyr, *The Second Apology*, pp. 125, 126.

16. Irenaeus, *Proof of the Apostolic Preaching*, Ancient Christian Writers, volume 16, The Newman Press, 1952, p. 107.

17. Athanasius, *Treatise on the Incarnation of the Word*, p. 322.

18. Augustine, pp. 316-317.

19. H. Noldin and A. Schmitt, S.J., *Summa Theologia Moralis*, volume 3, Innsbruck: Verlag, Felizian Rauch, 1960, Ques. 53, p. 42.

20. *Codex Iuris Canonici*, A.A.S. Westminster: Newman Bookshop, 1944, Canon 1151, pp. 385-386.

21. Noldin and Schmitt, *op. cit.*, Ques. 54, p. 43.

22. Alphonso Maria d'Ligouri, *Praxis Confessarii*, Augustae Taurimorum: H. Marietti, 1829, para. 113.

23. Adolphe Tanquery, *The Spiritual Life*, Rev. Herman Branderis, (trans.) Baltimore: St. Mary's Seminary, 1930, para. 1536, p. 720.

24. *Ibid.*, para. 1545, p. 725, cf. Lehmkuhl, *Theol. Moralis*, 1910 ed., t. 11, note 574.

25. Noldin and Schmitt, *op. cit.*, note 3, p. 43.

26. John McHugh and Charles J. Callan, O.P., *Moral Theology*, volume 2, New York: Joseph Wagner, 1958, para. 2267(b), p. 365.

27. Dominicus Prummer, *Manuale Theologiae Moralis II*, Barcelona: Herder: 1945, note 463, p. 384.

28. For guidelines for determining need for solemn exorcism, see Weller, *op. cit.*, pp. 641-644; Adolphe Tanquery. *The Spiritual Life*. Rev. Herman Branderis, (trans.) Baltimore: St. Mary's Seminary, 1930, paras. 1537-1543, pp. 720-723; Scanlan, *Prayers and Blessings from The Roman Ritual* with commentary by Michael Scanlan, TOR, private publication, College of Steubenville, 1978, pp. 25-26.

29. For further development of the sacraments and their effective utilization, see Michael Scanlan and Ann Therese Shields, *And Their Eyes Were Opened: Encountering Jesus in the Sacraments*, Ann Arbor: Servant Books, 1976.

30. For further discussion of sacramentals and their proper use, see Philip Weller, *The Roman Ritual*, Milwaukee: Bruce Publishing Co., 1964, pp. 384-391; *Prayers and Blessings*.

NEW TESTAMENT REFERENCES TO THE DEVIL

Devil, Satan, Spirits

Matthew
4:1-11
4:24
7:22
8:16
8:28-34
9:32-34
10:1
12:22-32
12:43
12:45
13:39
15:22
17:18
25:41

Mark
1:13
1:21-28
1:32
1:34
1:39
3:11
3:15
3:22-30
4:15
5:1-20
6:7
6:13
7:24-30
8:33
9:14-29
9:38
16:9
16:17

Luke
4:1-13
4:31-37
6:18
7:21
7:33
8:2
8:12
8:26-39
9:1
9:37-43
9:49
10:17-20
11:14-26
13:10-17
13:32
22:3
22:31

John
6:70
7:20
8:39-59
10:19-21
13:2
13:27

Acts
5:3
5:16
8:7
10:38
13:4-12
16:16-18
19:11-20
26:18

Romans
16:20

1 Corinthians
2:12
5:5
7:5
10:14-22
12:10

2 Corinthians
2:11
11:14
12:7

Ephesians
4:27
6:10-20

1 Thessalonians
2:18

2 Thessalonians
2:1-12

1 Timothy
1:20
3:6-7
4:1
5:15

2 Timothy
2:26

Hebrews
2:14

James
2:19
3:15
4:7

1 Peter
3:19
5:6-11

1 John
3:4-10
4:1
4:3

Jude
5-9

Revelation
2:(9)
2:(10)
2:13
2:24
3:9
9:20
12:1-17
16:(13-14)
18:2
20:1-10

Powers

Luke
22:53

Romans
8:38

1 Corinthians
15:24

Ephesians
2:2
3:10
6:12

Colossians
1:13
1:16
2:10
2:15

Hebrews
2:14
2:15

Revelation
13:2
13:4

Principalities

Ephesians
1:21

Rulers

John
12:31
14:30
16:11

1 Corinthians
2:6